WISDOM FOR ALL AGES

HAVE THE TIME
OF YOUR LIFE

GIOVANNI LIVERA

TIMECOMPASS, LLC
5703 Red Bug Lake Rd. #360
Winter Springs, FL 32708
888-855-7555 USA voice

TIMECOMPASS.com

ISBN # 0-9660567-4-4
Library of Congress Control # 2003112399

CREDITS
Developmental Editor: Ken Preuss
Editor: Christine Born
Cover Art and Illustrations: Michael Mojher
Text Design: Mimi Palladino Roberts

"Live A Thousand Years," "Sage Age," "YOUR-DASH,"
"The Twelve Chimes," and "Viva mille anni" are trademarks of
Giovanni Experiences, LLC.

10 9 8 7 6 5 4 3

⊶⟩⊙ ⊙⟩⊷

THIS BOOK BELONGS TO

MAY YOU LIVE A THOUSAND YEARS

For your family and mine.

✦ FOREWORD ✦

In 1998, I had the opportunity to see with my own eyes a performance that has been indelibly etched in my mind. It was an experience I will never forget.

The Amazing Giovanni captivated the hearts and minds of 700 professional speakers, which is a feat in and of itself. Whether it was fate, luck, magic, or divine inspiration, the next twelve months were the most successful period of my life and career. And it only continues to get better!

Giovanni Livera has a rare gift indeed. He is uniquely qualified and blessed with talent beyond his own imagination. His enthusiasm is contagious, and once in his presence, well, you'd better hang on for the ride.

Live A Thousand Years is truly his best work to date. It will touch your heart and engage your mind. Travel with Nick as he discovers The Twelve Chimes, and your life will never be the same.

This moment is for you. Read this book over and over and let the message sink into your heart, mind, and soul. I believe you will step into your potential in a way you only dreamed about before. It is my personal goal to get this book into the hands of one million readers. And after that, we'll find a few more.

As you will discover in reading this book, anything is possible, whether in your business, career, or your life!

Your time is now.

Mark LeBlanc

President of the National Speakers Association 2007-08

✛ INTRODUCTION ✛

"Dost thou love life?
Then do not squander time,
for that's the stuff life is made of."

BENJAMIN FRANKLIN

Most of us see the truth in Benjamin Franklin's famous quote, but few of us live it. I don't think we *purposely* squander time. It just happens. Many of us work so hard and so frantically that we're too weary to do much more than collapse in front of the TV each evening. We sleepwalk through our days, failing to savor the richness and color of life. Tragically, days, weeks, months and years slip through our fingers like sand, unnoticed and unappreciated. In short, *squandered*.

During my life, I have worked with everyone from no-nonsense CEOs to children awestruck by the appearance of a rabbit from a top hat. I have noticed that children have the edge on living in the moment. They don't live one second in the future or one second in the past. They experience full, passionate hours of playing, learning and truly experiencing this wonderful world. I've often asked myself: why does this sense of wonder have to drop away as we grow older?

The answer is that it doesn't. When you make the decision to live each hour to the fullest, life becomes a banquet of great splendor. No matter what dates are eventually carved on your tombstone, each hour you live can be a magnificent symphony where life is measured by moments and experiences, not clocks and calendars.

Take the message of this book to heart and I guarantee you will reawaken to, or perhaps even discover for the first time, a life and legacy filled with purpose, passion, pleasure, and peace.

May you live a thousand years,

Giovanni Livera

The MOMENT EVERYTHING CHANGED

NICK WAITES WAS RACING AT FULL TILT. UNFORTUNATELY, his cab was not. He glanced up from his watch and glared out the window. He had twelve minutes to get to his mid-day meeting, and he was caged in a big city traffic jam.

Turning away from the traffic that stretched before him, he closed his eyes and conjured up an image of a sinking shark: a majestic great white, plunging swiftly, almost elegantly, into the darkness of the sea. From the depths of his memory, he summoned his father's voice.

"A shark has to swim to survive," his father said. "If it stops moving, it sinks and dies."

Nick couldn't remember the original context of his father's words. Maybe he had been making up a story or reading a book. All Nick knew was that the image had stuck with him. Now, at age forty-three, he felt he and the shark had become kindred spirits, creatures that had to move continuously in order to survive.

Nick opened his eyes to assess the situation. The cab hadn't budged, and his driver had turned around almost completely to strike up a conversation.

"Don't know why we're so backed up," he said. "My guess is there's some kind of construction going on. Either that or an accident."

Nick nodded politely and looked at his watch. He didn't feel like talking which seemed to work out fine since the driver was having a wonderful conversation on his own.

"Nice watch. Antique? Bet it is. Don't see many passengers with pocket watches anymore. Never did, really." He paused for a breath and then laughed. "Course, I suppose, if they had'em, they'd have 'em hidden in their pockets, now wouldn't they?"

The driver opened his mouth to answer his own question. Nick opened his door to escape.

He tossed the man a twenty-dollar bill and crossed in front of the cab. In the short dash to the sidewalk, he could already feel his navy suit absorbing the heat of the sun. Nick loosened his tie and slid his watch into his pants pocket. It was 11:50. The café was three blocks away. He would make the rest of the journey by foot.

Nick headed south at a steady pace. He moved instinctively, weaving his way through the sea of pedestrians, reaching the first crosswalk just as the flashing signal changed to "walk".

Midway through the second block, Nick spotted a newspaper stand and decided to grab the daily business journal. He whistled ahead and caught the attention of a young man who sat, nearly napping, on a stool behind the counter. Without slowing his step, Nick picked up the paper, crammed it under his arm, whipped out a dollar, slapped it on the counter, and proceeded on his journey.

"What about your change?" the newspaper guy called after him.

Nick glanced back and shouted over his shoulder, "No time for change!"

Looking ahead again, he took a single step, then stopped, nearly falling forward. He was face-to-face with an old man standing directly in his path. A half a foot shorter and a good quarter of a century older, the man had wavy, white hair a gust of wind away from being completely out of control. A childlike grin emerged from within his thick, full beard and a gentle voice escaped.

"There's always time for change."

Not sure how to respond, Nick took a breath and caught sight of a clock in the storefront window. There were several clocks – actually, an entire store full. He stared at the faces and checked his watch to confirm what he saw. 11:55.

"Can't chat, old man," Nick said, sidestepping the curious fellow. "Not enough time."

The old man tipped an imaginary cap and gestured toward the shop. "I've got plenty," he said, stepping inside. "Stop by when things slow down."

Nick lifted his hand, acknowledging the invitation and waving it off at the same time. He broke into a semi-sprint with no intention of returning. The simple fact was, for Nick, things never did slow down.

Nick entered the final block of his journey feeling restless about the five minutes he would waste before he met his client. Remembering he needed to speak with his wife, he pulled his cell phone from his jacket and challenged himself to complete the call before he reached the corner. His feet moved swiftly, but his fingers froze on the speed dial.

Nick knew Alicia was at work. He pictured her at her desk, proofreading the novel by the young writer she had mentioned the evening before. He hadn't really been listening to her. His mind, as usual, had been on his own work. By the time he sensed the frustration in her voice, it was too late. Her frustration had shifted to anger. The evening ended in an uneasy, but not unfamiliar, silence. Nick shifted his finger to the button that dialed home. It would be easier to leave a message.

"Alicia, it's Nick. It looks like I'm going to be working late again. If you can get Grace to dance class, I'll do my best to pick her up on my way home. Got to go. Bye."

Nick hung up and looked down. He had reached the end of the message at the same time he had reached the end of the sidewalk. He crossed the intersection, hoping he hadn't reached the end of the marriage as well.

A small fence surrounded the outdoor café where he regularly met his clients. As he stepped through the lattice archway, he noticed flowers on the tables and made a mental note to buy some for Alicia on the way home. Taking a seat, he watched a young woman rush into the arms of a man entering behind him. He watched as they kissed passionately, thought of Alicia, and made another mental note.

Using a napkin to mop the sweat from his neck and brow, Nick ran his fingers through his thinning brown hair and breathed a sigh of relief. Though skinny, he was hardly in peak shape but he had made it on time. Pulling his watch from his pocket, he noticed the second hand move past the six. He had a full thirty seconds to spare. Marveling at his ability to master time, he closed his eyes for a moment – his version of quiet reflection. It was 11:59.

"It's time to move," he whispered in his standard pre-meeting pep talk. "You are the shark. Go for the kill."

Opening his eyes, he felt the presence of a waitress over his shoulder. He turned to catch her attention. Before he had the chance, the woman caught his. She stood completely still, as if frozen solid, in the act of pouring water for an equally motionless man. The bottle in her hand hovered above his glass with a trail of falling liquid stuck in midair.

Staring in disbelief, Nick was suddenly struck by the silence and stillness surrounding him. Turning wildly, he realized the entire café had come to a complete stop. He leapt to his feet and screamed in panic, getting nothing more than an echo in return.

"That's it," he thought. "I've done it. I've actually

lost my mind."

Checking his watch to commemorate the moment he'd gone mad, he realized it was still 11:59. The second hand had stopped one tick away from high noon.

He needed to move. Technically, everyone else needed to move, but since they didn't seem capable, he thought he would do the honors. Staggering toward the exit, he was blocked by the couple he had seen on his way in. They stood, framed in the archway, eyes closed, arms wrapped, lips connected, like a photograph in a wedding album.

Stumbling around them, Nick reached the sidewalk and stared at the street. The fact that the cars were not moving came as no surprise. Standstill traffic was a normal sight. What made the scene abnormal was the sound, or rather, the complete lack of it. Horns weren't honking. Radios weren't blaring. Motors weren't running. The entire city had simply stalled.

Passengers sat still in the seats of their cars. Pedestrians posed like statues on the sidewalks. A pack of business people stood halfway through the intersection, trapped in mid-step, as if they had been surprised by a flashing "don't walk" sign and had taken the warning far too literally.

Nick sprinted north, frantically retracing the path he had covered moments before. He scanned the streets, searching for a sign to help explain what was happening. He had traveled a block when he found it.

A large clock sign rotated slowly on a silver pole – the only movement in an otherwise immobile city. Nick's eyes widened as he read the words painted across its face: The Time Keeper.

The MYSTERY of the MAN in the SHOP

NICK STARED AT THE SIGN AS HE MOVED CLOSER TO the building. Two pigeons were motionless in the air above the store frozen in flight inches away from their destination. Nick, in contrast, flew steadily toward his. Befuddled, he wondered, "Why is whole city frozen except for me and the clock shop's sign?"

Reaching the front of the shop, he hesitated, certain he was meant to enter, but uncertain of what he would find. Pushing his way in, he heard a brass bell on the door announce his entrance. As it quieted,

Nick heard the one thing he had hoped he wouldn't – silence.

The shop was stocked with clocks of every shape and size, yet not a single one among the dusty shelves was making noise. Every one of them was frozen on the same time – 11:59.

"You're back!"

Nick was startled. Turning toward the sound, he discovered the peculiar man he had met earlier. He sat in the shadow of a grandfather clock with an assortment of fishing lures scattered on the counter before him. There was a spark of enthusiasm in his wizened, hazel eyes and warmth in the wrinkles bordering them. His right hand rose and waved hello; His left hand twisted the curls of his handlebar mustache.

"The name's Maximillion," he offered. "My friends call me Max."

Nick responded without realizing he was speaking aloud. "You ... you can move?"

"Of course I can move," he replied playfully. "I'm old, but I'm not dead." The man tucked a locket into the collar of his shirt and began placing the lures into the pockets of his golden vest. "Was toying with the idea of going fishing," he said. "It's been a little slow around here today."

"A little slow?" Nick exclaimed, moving to the edge of the counter. "Have you looked at your clocks?"

"Many times."

Nick lost patience. He grabbed his pocket watch and placed it on the counter in front of the shopkeeper. If it had not had sentimental value, he would have slammed it.

Max gave the watch a quick glance. "What seems to be the trouble?"

"The trouble? The trouble is that the world as we know it has come to a stop, and you're thinking about going fishing!"

Max ignored Nick's outburst and took the watch in his hands. "I mean, what's the trouble with the watch?"

"My watch stopped at 11:59. Everything else, except you, seemed to stop with it."

"I see." Max gave the watch a closer look. "This is nice. Where'd you get it?"

Nick collapsed on a stool. Too exhausted to battle for control of the conversation, he decided to play along until he could regain the advantage.

"It was a gift from my grandfather," Nick explained. "He left it to me when he died."

"It's in great shape. An old railway piece, you know?"

"Yeah. Granddad was pretty proud of it. He always said it was quite a watch. What he didn't say was that if I forgot to wind it, all of creation would screech to a halt."

Max turned it over and read an inscription off the back. "'For Nicholas.' That you?"

"It was. I mean, it is." Nick rubbed his temples to try and straighten his thoughts. "I go by Nick. My grandfather called me Nicholas. No one's called me that since he died."

"He died when you were young?"

Nick shook his head. "He was around most of my life. He helped raise me with my mother when my dad left. Granddad died about ten years back."

"Well, it must have made him happy to have

someone to pass the watch on to."

"Yeah. Well, he didn't actually pass it on ... "

Nick's voice trailed as his emotions began to take hold. Though the words stopped, the memories came flooding in ... The phone call concerning his grandfather's condition ... His promise to fly home as soon as possible ... The sales call that made him miss the flight. He flashed ahead to the day of the funeral, and was saddened by how clearly he recalled the events.

He stood in his mother's house, in the small bedroom where he spent his childhood. He was fastening his tie when the mirror showed his mother stepping through the doorway behind him. For a fleeting moment, he felt like a child getting ready for church. He turned, half-expecting his mother to hug him as she had every Sunday for so many years. Instead, she walked past him and set a pocket watch on the dresser. Her eyes met his in the reflection of the glass. Her words cut him deeply. "Your granddad wanted to give this to you in person. You should have come home sooner."

She left the room without saying another word
and never mentioned the watch again. Nick had
carried it with him ever since, often wondering what
his grandfather might have said in that moment they
never shared.

"You okay, son?"

Max's voice pulled Nick back to the present.
Seeing the watch reminded him that the present time
was still 11:59. He shook off the sadness and spoke.

"So? Can you fix the watch?"

"Nope."

"Why not?"

"It's not broken."

"Not broken? Have you seen what it's like out
there?"

Max slid the watch back and stood. "It's a nice
watch, Nick. A wonderful family heirloom. But it
didn't stop the universe."

"How do you know?"

"Because *I* stopped the universe."

As Max turned and walked with a sense of
purpose toward a draped doorway, Nick called

after him.

"What do you mean? I don't understand."

"Relax," Max said, reaching for the curtain. "I'll explain everything. We've got all the time in the world."

ALL the TIME in the WORLD

NICK SLIPPED HIS WATCH INTO HIS POCKET AS he stood.

"You're telling me you have the ability to stop time?"

Max nodded casually as if the idea were of no particular interest. Drawing back the curtain, he disappeared into the darkness of the next room.

"How'd you do it then?" Nick shouted.

The response came in the form of an invitation.

"Step back here. I'll show you."

For the first time since he had entered the eccentric man's shop, Nick felt a rush of excitement. Making his way to the back room, he tried to imagine what he was about to see. As his eyes adjusted to the darkness, he envisioned a machine: a mechanical apparatus of cosmic significance, an intricate assembly of swinging pendulums, spinning wheels, and shining lights.

What he found was a giant hourglass.

It was the largest one he had ever seen, too large to fit through a door, but it was in no other way extraordinary. A simple design of curved glass and unfinished wood, it rested sideways on the floor so that the tiny grains of sand sat motionless within the glass.

"You look disappointed."

"I was expecting something a little more elaborate."

Max patted the side of the glass. "She may not look like much," he said, "but she works like a dream."

"So this is a whole 'Sands of Time' thing then?" Nick asked, running his hands along the glass. "You stand this baby on its end and time starts flowing. You lay it sideways, the sand settles and time stops."

"That's pretty much it."

"And you just stop time whenever you want?"

"I never *want* to stop time. I *have* to. It's part of my job."

"And what *is* your job exactly?"

Max responded slowly as if surprised by Nick's inquiry. "I'm the Time Keeper." He cracked a smile. "Didn't you read the sign out front?"

Nick ignored the question and asked another of his own. "So, what were you doing that forced you to stop time?"

"I was taking inventory. Adding new grains. Releasing old ones. Balancing things out."

Nick nodded as if he understood, his mind still searching for meaning, his eyes still looking for clues. Leaning over, he stared at the sand that lay still within the hourglass. "So, what do all these grains represent then? Days? Hours?"

"People."

"People?"

"One grain per person. I stop the sand. The people stop with it."

"But I'm still moving!" Nick exclaimed, turning his

attention to the old man. "How do you explain that?"

"Simple. I took you out."

"You did what?"

"I took you out."

Max reached forward and pulled open a tiny, transparent window that sat virtually invisible in the top half of the glass. He placed his hand in the hourglass so his fingers dangled just above the sand. "I was working in the sand, and I just plucked you out with a pair of tweezers." Max mimed the actions playfully, then pulled his hand from the sand timer.

"Why did you do it?"

"We needed to talk. I mentioned that to you when you nearly ran me over. I could see that you weren't going to make the time, so I facilitated it myself."

"Facilitated it? You plucked me out of there with a pair of tweezers! That's not facilitating, that's … kidnapping!"

"Kidnapping? You walked into my shop on your own. You can walk out whenever you want. All I did was create a chance for us to chat."

Nick thought about this for a minute — or at least for what might have been a minute if time had been progressing normally. He moved back to the sand timer and stared at the tiny grains.

"So, you're telling me that everyone, aside from me, is in this thing?"

Max leaned and looked with him. "Everyone. Your mother. Your father. Your wife and daughter."

"What about my grandfather?"

"He's in here, yes, but he's on this side." Max moved to the opposite end of the hourglass. "He's already passed through."

"Passed through?"

"There are two sides to the sand timer. When I stand this back up, everyone heads in the same direction."

"So everyone on the bottom side has … ?"

"Passed through. Gone to the other side."

"Died."

"Everyone dies, Nick. The question is, how many people actually live?"

"What's that supposed to mean?"

"Just what I hoped we could chat about. Allow

me to illustrate."

Max patted his vest as if searching for something he needed. After a few failed attempts, he placed his hand in a pocket and pulled out a small spiral notebook. He paused again as if forgetting something else, then grabbed a pen from behind his ear.

Nick shook his head at the man's antics and followed him to a worktable in the corner. As they sat down, Nick watched Max's shaky hand scratch out a sketch of a tombstone. With the picture complete, Max printed the words "Your Name Here" where the name of the deceased would have been.

"When you die," Max explained, "someone will carve your tombstone. They will carve your birth date and your death date separated by a single dash." He drew as he spoke, substituting question marks in lieu of actual numbers. Setting the notebook down, he slid the sketch to Nick.

"Look at it closely for a moment."

Nick did as Max asked. Staring at the drawing, he slowly envisioned his own name on the tombstone. He pictured his birth date carved to the left of the dash and his death date carved to the right. He toyed with guessing when that death might actually come, but was glad when his thoughts were interrupted.

"There are a lot of carvings on that tombstone," Max began. "Which is the most important?"

"The death date." Nick chuckled nervously. "You want it as far off as possible."

Max looked directly into Nick's eyes. "The dash." He took the notebook and pointed with the pen for emphasis. "It's what's between the dates that's most important. Focus on the dash. The dash represents your life."

"I never thought about it like that before."

"Well, now you know why I wanted to chat."

"So you can tell me about the dash?"

"I can teach you how to get more out of it."

"I'm doing fine, thanks," Nick said, feeling a bit offended. "I have a career. I have a family. The way I see it, I'm gonna be a millionaire. I don't think my dash is going too badly."

"No, it's just going too fast."

"And you're going to teach me how to slow

things down?"

"Even better," Max said, returning the notebook to a vest pocket. "I'm going to show you how to live a thousand years."

The SECRET of SAGE AGE

NICK WAS STILL TRYING TO MAKE SENSE OF MAX'S words when the old man removed a calculator from his vest. Max patted his pockets in an attempt to locate something else, then snatched out a small black book.

"If my memory serves me correctly," Max muttered as he flipped through the pages, "your grandfather's full name was Vincent Tomaselli."

"You knew my granddad?"

"Just by name. I know everybody by name. It's

one of the perks of the job. The book helps me keep track of everything else."

"You have information about everyone in that book?"

"Everyone that is and was."

"How does all that information fit in such a tiny book?"

Max looked up. "Can you keep a secret?"

Nick nodded eagerly.

"So can I." Max winked and returned his focus to the tattered book. "Ah, yes! Here he is." He grabbed the calculator with his free hand and began punching buttons. After a few moments, he stopped and glanced at his results.

"I don't get it," Nick exclaimed. "What did you just do?"

Max slipped the book back into his vest pocket and gave Nick a satisfied grin. "I just figured out how long your grandfather lived."

"I could have told you that. He was eighty-two."

"Actually, he was five hundred and twenty-five."

Max slid the calculator over to Nick. Nick looked

at the number: 525.

"What did you do? Multiply like dog years? Mom and I considered granddad a saint, but he wasn't a Saint Bernard." Nick slid the calculator back toward Max. "I don't see how this number can be right."

"Then you've got to learn to look at things differently." Max turned the calculator 180 degrees and slid it back so that Nick was forced to read it upside-down. Once again, it read 525.

"That's a cute trick, but there's no way my grandfather lived to be five hundred and twenty-five."

"He could have lived to be a thousand."

"You're crazy."

"You come in here claiming that your watch controls the universe, and I'm the one who's crazy?"

"It's not possible for a person to live to be a thousand years old."

"According to *your* math, maybe."

"*My* math? Oh, I see. You have your own math?"

"I do."

"Well, you have your own science ... with the whole 'stopping time' thing. So why not have your own math? You know what? If you go back and create your own history, everything I learned in school will be rendered completely useless!"

"Nothing you learn is ever useless."

Nick rolled his eyes, weary of the conversation. "This is deep. Should I be writing these pearls of wisdom down?"

"Well, you shouldn't be *putting* them down." Max was visibly annoyed by Nick's sarcasm. "I'm doing this for your benefit, not mine. If you'd like to leave, I'd be happy to show you to the door."

Nick was startled by the seriousness of the old man's words. "Okay," he said, "I'm trying to understand. I just don't get what you did with the calculator." He rubbed his temples and refocused. "Explain to me how my grandfather lived to be five hundred and twenty-five."

"Five hundred and twenty-five was his Sage Age."

"His Sage Age?"

"The years that he lived multiplied by how wisely he lived them."

"Why are you multiplying anything? What's

wrong with real age?"

"Age is a linear concept, Nick. It measures how long you've existed and nothing more. Life is a grand endeavor. It should be measured by moments, not hours; by experiences, not years."

"And Sage Age does all that?"

"All that and more. Sage Age is a measurement of quality. It reveals how successfully you are living your life, how wisely you are making your dash."

"So, I can make my dash longer?"

"Yes, if you take care of yourself. But the key is to make your dash thicker! You can expand it with meaningful life experiences. If you can learn to live by The Twelve Chimes, it is possible to gain the life experience of a thousand years."

Nick sighed, wanting to follow along, but finding it difficult to do so. "What exactly are The Twelve Chimes?"

Max raised his eyebrows and turned away. Leading Nick to a door on the back wall, he opened it to reveal a long, dark tunnel. Nick stared into the blackness, failing to see any sign of light.

"What's through there?"

"Watch."

"Watch what?"

"Watch," repeated Max, this time extending an open palm.

"I *am* watching."

"I'm asking you for your watch. Place it in my hand."

Nick gave an embarrassed laugh and did as Max asked. Max held the watch up so that Nick could see it clearly.

"Right now, you take time at face value. When you look at this watch, all you see are the numbers. It's time you learned the meaning behind them."

Max twisted the watch and removed the crystal protecting the face. Nick responded in a near panic.

"What are you doing? That's not supposed to come off!"

"Neither are these." Max ran his hand over the front of the watch and the numbers magically jumped into his closing fist. "Numbers to you are just minutes, hours, and dollars. You have no respect for them."

He turned to the door, opened his palm, and blew the tiny digits into the darkness.

Nick was wonderstruck. "What did you do?"

"I sent them away."

"Why?"

"So you can earn them back."

"How do I do that?"

"One number at a time."

Max placed the crystal cover back on the watch and handed it to Nick. Max snatched a charcoal-colored overcoat from a hook on the wall, slipped it on, and stepped through the doorway. Nick watched him vanish into the abyss, hesitated, then called after him.

"What do you want me to do?"

The old man's voice came back as if he had already traveled a great distance. "Follow me! We're going to Chime One!"

The
INEXPLICABLE
AUCTION

NICK STEPPED IN AND HEARD THE DOOR SLAM SOLIDLY behind him. Enveloped by darkness, he called out again and received nothing in response but an echo. He stretched out his arms and searched in every direction, hoping to find a wall to guide him. Finding none, Nick walked forward for several yards until sounds let him know that he was not alone.

In front of him, there was a squeak of someone adjusting a seat. To his right, he heard a solid object hitting a wooden surface. To his left began a strange, high-pitched whir of what he assumed to be some sort of wheel spinning.

Concerned for his safety, Nick made a plea into the darkness. "Can I get some light in here?"

His request was greeted with the flash of a spotlight. The white-hot glare pierced the darkness and Nick threw his hands up to shade his eyes. Realizing he was on a stage, he addressed a group of shadowy figures assembled in rows before him.

"What's going on? Who are you?"

His words were drowned by a sudden noise.

BAM! BAM!

He turned to his right and spied a thin figure in the spill of the spotlight. The bony fingers of his left hand tap-danced on the edge of a lectern. His right hand lifted a gavel high above his head and brought it crashing down again.

BAM! BAM! BAM!

As the sound reverberated in Nick's ears, he became aware of the thin man's voice. Manic and menacing, it commanded the attention of the entire room.

"Ladies and gentlemen," he began, "the auction is now underway."

Footlights flickered from the edge of the stage and an eerie, candle-like glow emerged. As the crowd began to murmur, Nick turned, expecting to find an assortment of merchandise standing behind him. He was startled to see nothing but his own shadow, enlarged by the light and pinned to the back wall.

He took a step toward the lectern to demand an explanation when the auctioneer snatched Nick's right arm and lifted it forcibly into the air.

"First up on the block. An arm! Let's start the bidding at one hundred thousand dollars." Nick tried to pull away. The auctioneer tightened his grip and continued, "Do I hear one hundred thousand?"

A shadowy figure in the audience raised a wooden paddle to indicate his bid. "One hundred thousand!" A second paddle appeared at the opposite end of the auditorium. "Two hundred thousand!"

"Two hundred thousand for the arm!" the auctioneer smiled. "Do I hear three hundred?"

Nick wrenched his arm from the man's grasp.

He ran a few steps to his left then stopped. Three figures stood in the wings, shoulder to shoulder, blocking his path. Unlike the anonymous shadows in the crowd, the trio had a more obvious and sinister purpose. Dressed in scrubs and peering from behind surgical masks, they were doctors awaiting an operation. The first held a scalpel. The second held a saw. The third held an unusually long knife, sharpening it against the wheel that Nick had heard in the darkness.

Turning back toward the podium, Nick swung his right arm and pointed. "Are they for real?"

The auctioneer ignored the question and addressed the crowd. "You see that, folks? A fully serviceable arm. It stretches *and* points!"

The auctioneer reached for Nick's arm a second time, but Nick avoided his grasp. Unfazed, the man simply worked it into the sales pitch. "What it lacks in muscular development, it makes up for in speed and agility!"

The crowd was obviously impressed.

"Four hundred thousand!"

"Five hundred!"

"Stop!"

Nick's arm shot upward, fingers spread. Though it brought the auction to a halt, he realized the dramatic gesture had probably increased the value of his arms.

The auctioneer lowered his voice and addressed Nick one on one. "What's the problem?"

Nick stepped closer, remaining cautious in case the man attempted to grab him again. "You can't sell my arm."

"Why not?"

"I won't give you the right."

"Then give me the left."

"What?"

"The left arm. The right one's obviously the dominant one. What do you use the left arm for anyway? To hold the toast while you butter it? To scrape peas onto your fork? Let me sell it. You won't even miss it."

"Where is Max? He said he was going to help me."

"You said you're going to be a millionaire, right?"

"Yeah, but ... "

The thin man turned away quickly and addressed the crowd, "Do I hear one million dollars for the left arm?"

"One million!"

"Sold!"

BAM!

Nick flinched. The crowd murmured. The auctioneer leaned over and whispered again.

"If you worked out a little more, I could've gotten you two million."

Nick was about to respond when he heard a sound from the wings. It was the whir of the sharpening wheel shifting to a higher speed. He turned and glanced, and though he could not be sure, he sensed the trio had moved a bit closer.

"On to our next item," the auctioneer announced. "Next up, an eye!"

Nick buried his face in his hands in disbelief, only to have the auctioneer swat them away.

"Don't hide the merchandise, son. I'm trying to make you some cash." He grabbed Nick's chin and turned his face toward the crowd. "Look at these eyes, ladies and gentlemen. Bloodshot? Yes. But a beautiful shade of blue."

Paddles shot up throughout the audience.

"One million!"

"One million five!"

"I'm not selling an eye!" Nick protested, his chin still within the man's grasp.

"Relax," the auctioneer muttered, slightly tightening his grip. "You've got two of 'em!"

"One million eight!"

"One million nine!"

"The eyes, folks. The 'windows to the soul.' The left one or the right one ... your choice."

"Two million!"

"Sold!"

BAM!

The auctioneer let go of Nick's chin and patted him on the top of his head. His playful gesture turned painful as he pressed down hard and palmed Nick's skull like a basketball.

"Ladies and gentlemen ... our final item: The brain!"

The crowd cheered wildly. The surgeons stepped closer. The spotlight bounced off their blades.

The auctioneer leaned toward Nick, raising his voice to be heard above the frenzy. "What will you take for your brain, son? Five million? Ten million?"

"You can't sell them my brain."

"Why not?"

"Because I'll die."

"We're all gonna die sometime. You could die a rich man!"

"But I want to live!"

"Then live!"

This response came not from the auctioneer, but from a member of the audience. Booming loudly from a back row, it took everyone in the auditorium by surprise. A silhouette rose from a seat, and Nick knew it at once to be that of Maximillion.

Max thrust his arms outward, and the audience members disappeared into thin air. They vanished rapidly, one row after the next, their abandoned paddles crashing to the floor in a furious wave of sound.

He pointed forward and the trio of surgeons

disappeared in the same manner. Their instruments fell violently, the saw and scalpel ricocheting in opposite directions, the knife sticking, blade-first, into the wooden stage, inches away from Nick's feet.

With a third and final gesture, Max dispensed of the auctioneer. The gavel, no longer in his grasp, struck the ground with an ominous finality, like a hammer driving the final spike into a coffin.

For a moment, Nick heard nothing but the beating of his own heart. When he became aware of Max's footsteps heading toward the stage, Nick's fear subsided and anger crept in to fill the void.

"What was that all about?"

"You didn't enjoy the lesson?"

"I didn't get the point."

Max pulled the knife out of the floor and waved the blade. "You nearly got this one."

"Watch it!" Nick stumbled back and began to pace. "What was the deal with those guys wanting to dissect me?"

"Your arms. Your eyes. Your brain. Are they connected?"

Nick pointed to the tools. "They wouldn't be if I had let them use those."

"Each of them represents something about you, Nick. The arms are an extension of your body. The eyes are the windows to the soul. The brain is the instrument of intellect."

Nick shrugged, unable to see the meaning, unwilling to even try.

Max pointed to his own body, moving from his arm, to his eyes, to his head. "The physical, the spiritual, and the mental. These are the things that make us who we are."

"That's why I was trying to hold on to them during your little lesson."

"You looked out for yourself during the auction, but you need to do that in real life as well. You must take care of yourself ... physically, spiritually, and mentally."

Nick sneered. "Exercise. Attend church. Do a crossword puzzle. Got it."

Max frowned at the flippant remark. "It's a bit more serious than that."

Nick sighed and sat down on the edge of the

stage. "I'm sorry. I still don't understand. I thought you were going to teach me about life experience."

"It's simple, Nick. The longer you live, the more opportunities you have to gain experience."

Nick let the words sink in for a moment then shook his head and sighed.

"I just don't have a lot of time for myself. I have to work. I have to make money. I have to support my family."

"You don't *have* to, Nick. You *get* to. Everything you do is worth enjoying."

Max moved to the curtain at the side of the stage and pulled it back to reveal a large antique cash register. He pounded his fingers across the brass keys and called out over the clicks and rattle of the machine.

"A million dollars for an arm. Two million for an eye!" He paused to consult the paper receipt feeding from the register. "According to my calculations, you're already a multimillionaire. And with your mind, you're priceless."

Max cupped a hand behind his ear and hit the

total button. He smiled at the sound that accompanied the action.

"Did you hear that?"

Nick replied, "The register's bell? What about it?"

"The bell lets us know when you're ready."

"Ready for what?"

"This."

Max ripped the receipt from the top of the cash register and presented it to Nick with a flourish. "Chime One reminds you to take care of number one. Take care of the most valuable thing you have: You. Hold your watch and read the paper out loud."

Nick took his watch into his hand, frowning slightly as he saw the numberless face. Glancing at the receipt, he found it numberless as well. Words were printed where he had expected to see digits. He took a deep breath and read.

⊸⊃ CHIME 1 ⊂⊶

TIME FOR YOURSELF

I make personal time for myself.
I invest time to improve my health.
I manage my overall stress.
I act like the individual I want to become.

Max plucked the receipt from Nick's hand and pointed toward the watch. Nick saw the number one slowly begin to reappear. As the number reclaimed its position on the watch's face, a smile returned to Nick's.

Max pocketed the receipt and moved away.

Nick felt a rush of enthusiasm. He leapt from the stage and followed. "What's next?"

"You'll get to find out on your own," Max said, walking toward the back of the auditorium. "I will tell you this, though: It lies behind one of these."

Max pointed toward two wooden doors on the back wall. Nick placed the watch in his pocket and followed, wondering which one he should choose.

The RIGHT DOORS

Nᴉᴄᴋ sᴛᴏᴏᴅ ʙᴇꜰᴏʀᴇ ᴛʜᴇ ʟᴀʀɢᴇ, ᴀʀᴄʜᴇᴅ ᴅᴏᴏʀᴡᴀʏs admiring their construction. The solid wood planks and iron strap hinges seemed straight out of a medieval castle. Max placed a hand on Nick's shoulder and spoke.

"Pick one."

"Which one will get us where we need to go?"

"Either one will get us someplace."

Nick pulled the left door, struggling slightly with its heaviness. Glancing in, he saw a solid staircase leading downward. He pulled the door to the right to reveal a similar staircase heading up.

"Well?" asked Max.

"Well, the auction wore me out a bit. I suppose it'll be easier if we head down."

"Let's go then."

The twosome traveled steadily and silently down a single flight of stairs until they came to a pair of doors, identical to the ones they had just seen. Nick turned and looked back. The steps they had just descended were gone.

"What just happened?"

"You made a choice."

"What now?"

"You choose again."

Nick looked at the doors. Centered directly between them was a small, wooden sign with four painted words.

Nick leaned forward and read the sign aloud,"'Choose the right door'?" He thought for a moment, then turned to Max. "Does that mean 'choose the correct door' or 'choose the door on the right'?"

"What do you think?"

"I think you should just tell me so we don't waste any more time."

"You get to figure this one out on your own."

"You're not going to help at all?"

"I'll help a little." Max pulled the doors open revealing two stairways configured as before. "Up or down?"

"It would be easier if you told me where we were supposed to go."

Max laughed. "But it wouldn't be nearly as much fun, and besides, is 'easy' your goal?"

Nick sighed at the stairways. "Well, we've already come down one flight. No use going back up now."

"Lead the way then."

Nick stepped through the door on the left and headed down the stairs. Reaching the bottom, he found himself staring, once again, at an identical pair of doors. He looked back, saw that the stairs he had taken had vanished, and let out a sigh of frustration. "Is this supposed to be teaching me something?"

"Everything teaches you something, Nick. Choose

to be ready."

"I was ready two flights ago. Now I'm just tired."

"Choose again."

"It's a bit redundant, isn't it?"

"No matter where you are in life, you always have two options. A negative one and a positive one. No matter how low you go, no matter how many bad choices you make, no matter who you are, you always have two choices. There is always hope." Max touched the door on the left, and the word *Negadoor* appeared above it. He touched the door on the right, and created the word *Posidoor*. "Does that make it easier for you to choose?"

"I'm supposed to choose 'the right one' — the positive door. That's the point of your little exercise. Correct?"

Max offered no response. Nick pulled open the door and eyed the stairs without enthusiasm.

"Your little exercise is giving me a little too much exercise. Come on. Let's get it over with."

Nick moved up the stairs, breathing a bit more heavily. When he reached the top, he stopped and stared at another pair of doors.

"You've got to be kidding!"

"What's wrong now?"

"I'm tired of this."

"Aren't you the man who wants to be moving at all times?"

"But I'm not getting anywhere!"

"Of course you are. Every choice you make brings you closer to something or somewhere. You are the sum of all your choices. You create your path one flight at a time. One day at a time. One choice at a time."

"So, everything is a choice. If I make the positive choice, I'll get to a positive place, right?" Nick questioned.

"Right."

"Great. What do I do now?"

"Choose."

"But I already got it! I went up that time! I chose the right door!"

Max shook his head. "You went in the right direction, but you went with the wrong attitude."

"What's attitude got to do with it?"

"Attitude is a choice, too, Nick. You can choose to have a positive one or a negative one. Attitude is a powerful choice. When you approach each day with a positive attitude, there is a greater likelihood that you will make other positive choices."

Nick opened the door on the right and took a deep breath. "Positive choices. Positive attitude."

"Now, that'll get you places."

"Let's move then."

Nick headed up the stairs with a new sense of determination. When he reached the next set of doors, he paused to catch his breath, then headed through the one on the right.

Max followed with a smile. "What are you thinking?"

"Positive thoughts!" Nick answered, his eyes focused forward.

"Like what?"

"Like sooner or later, one of these Posidoors will lead me into an elevator with a tall glass of water!"

"No need," Max laughed. "Once you start making positive choices, it becomes easier."

Nick realized that Max was right. His momentum was building. He was definitely climbing at a quicker pace than he had been the flight before. Reaching the top of the stairs, he headed directly through the Posidoor. He climbed the flight, glancing back occasionally to watch the stairs dissolve behind them.

Max called forward as he kept pace, "Have you figured out why the stairs disappear?"

Nick gave the question some thought. "Once you make a choice, you can't go back," Nick said as he reached the top of the flight. "You can only make another choice."

Nick pulled open another Posidoor and continued his climb. At the top of the next floor, he flung open the door and stopped suddenly at an unexpected sight.

A wooden spiral staircase towered before him in a dangerous state of disrepair. Suspended by a series of worn ropes, the incline was unusually steep. A majority of the steps seemed to be fastened poorly or snapped in two. Others were missing completely. Nick looked up tentatively then leaped back as a large section of railing snapped loose and crashed to the floor beside him. He turned toward his companion and raised an eyebrow.

"This one looks a little dangerous."

"The right choice isn't always the easy one."

Max moved to the left and opened the Negadoor. He pointed to a solid stairway heading safely downward, covered with comfortable red carpeting. "Maybe we should choose to go this way."

"Oh, no," Nick laughed. "We're not going to turn back now." He pushed the Negadoor shut and pointed right. "We can do this. Think positive."

Max pretended to protest. "There are falling pieces and missing stairs. What are we supposed to do about that?"

Nick picked up a fragment of the railing and set it where the second step should have been. "We turn the negatives into positives. We use the fallen pieces to bridge the gaps." He walked to the third step and beckoned Max to follow. When they were standing side by side, Nick leaned back and lifted the railing. "We'll just carry it with us until we need it again."

They traveled the remainder of the stairway in

the same way, steadily making their way to the top. Nick set the railing in place of the final step, made his way to solid ground, then extended his hand to help Max do the same. Looking exhausted, Max leaned against Nick. He breathed heavily and spoke.

"That was an effort."

Nick gave a deep sigh of accomplishment. "That was an adventure."

Still supporting Max, Nick turned his head toward the two new doors. A large grandfather clock stood in the space between them.

"This is where we are supposed to be."

"Are you sure?" Max panted, with a smile.

Nick patted his companion on the back, "I'm *positive*."

The grandfather clock chimed. Max smiled and stood straight. He regained his stamina so quickly that Nick wondered if the weariness had simply been a ruse.

"That's a chime. Does that mean I'm ready for the second lesson?" Nick asked.

"It does. Chime Two reminds you that in everything

you think and do, you always have two choices. When you make positive choices, you move up in your life. When you make negative ones, you move down. You are the sum of the choices you make. Choose the positive."

Max pointed to the Posidoor. Nick lifted a paper door hanger off the knob. Removing his watch from his pocket, he took a breath and read.

⊷ CHIME 2 ⊷

TIME TO BE POSITIVE

I choose a positive attitude.
I make positive choices in my life.
I see the potential in others.
I see possibilities in negative situations.

Nick held the door hanger outward as if to ask what to do with it. Max took it and slid it into another side pocket. Nick glanced at his watch and saw the second digit appear. He held the watch out for Max to see. "I got it."

"Let's keep going then."

Nick's eyes sparkled as he flung open the Posidoor. Flights of stairs led up to wide-open doors as far as his eyes could see. "Look! I can see my whole path!"

Max put a hand on Nick's shoulder. "Nick," he said, "when your mind is aligned with the positive, all the right doors are open for you."

Nick gestured to the stairs. "To Chime Three then?"

"To Chime Three," Max nodded. "Why don't we take the express route?"

He moved toward the grandfather clock and opened the tall, glass door that stood within its frame. Max winked at Nick and gestured.

"After you."

The Gift

NICK STEPPED THROUGH THE DOOR OF THE grandfather clock and entered a large room cluttered with mirrors, mannequins, and sewing machines. Max stepped out of the clock and stood beside him.

"What is this place?"

"The back room of a tailor's shop," explained Max. "Phil and Ann Thropy. Charming couple. You'll like them." He cupped his hands and gave a little yell. "Anyone work in this place? Can we get a little service?"

A balding head peeked through the doorway of a distant wall. Seconds later, a short, round man with a beaming grin came waddling toward them. He was shadowed by a slender woman with bushy red hair and wire-rim glasses. Max extended his hand and greeted them.

"Phil, old pal. It's been a while."

Phil shook Max's hand vigorously. "Good to see you, you old rascal. Been fishing lately?"

"Been wanting to."

"You should have seen the whopper I caught last weekend." He spread his hands, demonstrating the size. "Four feet at least."

Ann pushed Phil's hands closer together. "You'd think that a man who measured things for a living would be a little more accurate with estimates." She laughed and gave Max a hug. "Jacket holding up for you? We put enough pockets in it, didn't we?"

"It's perfect, Ann. Just what I ordered. I'm here for my new friend, Nick."

She turned her head and noticed Nick for the first time. "Oh! Forgive me for being so rude, dear.

My name's Ann. My husband and I run the shop."
She tapped her husband on the shoulder, "Introduce
yourself."

Phil turned toward Nick and extended his hand,
"I'm Phil."

Nick reached out to shake hands. Phil slipped
him a coat hanger.

"What's this for?" Nick asked.

"I'm not sure where you come from, young man,
but around these parts, we use them to hang up our
clothes." Phil tried to keep a straight face, but burst
out in a hearty laugh. Max laughed along with him.
Ann shook her head and gave Nick a comforting
smile.

"Just hang your jacket on it, honey."

Nick paused thoughtfully. "What are we doing,
exactly?"

Ann opened her mouth to give a reply, but
realized she didn't have one. She called to Max as he
made his way to a seat across the room, "What are we
doing, exactly?"

He answered without looking back, "The usual."

Ann relayed the response to Nick, "The usual."

Nick sighed and hung up his jacket. "Why do I have the feeling that the usual is going to end up being unusual?"

Ann placed the hanger on a hook and moved to a worktable where she began spreading material.

Phil stepped into Nick's line of view. "Stand up straight now," he said. "We'll have you fitted in a jiffy."

He stretched a tape measure across the length of Nick's arm and called out a measurement. Ann repeated it, snatched up a pair of scissors, and began cutting. The process continued with precision. The stretch of the tape, the shout of measurements, and the snap of the scissors echoed through the shop like music until Phil flung his hands into the air.

"Finished!"

As Ann echoed him from across the room, Phil led Nick to three full-length mirrors with beautiful bronze frames. "Ann will be right here."

Nick looked at himself for the first time since the entire ordeal began. He viewed himself from the front and from the sides. He looked a little tired. His hair was less styled than he liked. But for a man who had survived the stoppage of time, nearly lost a limb, and sprinted up several flights of vanishing stairs, he didn't look half bad. He flashed a confident smile and caught a glimpse of Max relaxing in a cushioned chair, flipping through a fishing magazine.

Nick turned to address him but stopped when Ann stepped into view. She carried a bright red sports coat. The fabric seemed foreign yet familiar at the same time.

Nick squinted to get a better look. "Is that ... paper?"

"Wrapping paper," she responded. "Arms back, so I can slip it on." She helped him into the jacket, and turned him back toward the mirror. She moved in front of him, smoothing out the lapels, then stepped aside and gestured to the mirror as if showing off her work.

"What do you think, Nick?"

"It feels sort of funny. I ... " Nick stopped as he looked up into the glass. Though he wore the jacket on his body, it did not appear in any of the three mirrors before him. He touched his hand to his chest and crinkled the paper with his fingertips. However, the three mirrors reflected only him grabbing his shirt.

Ann moved behind Nick and joined hands with Phil. Nick watched them in the glass, then looked at his reflection again, trying to figure out what was going on. "This is an 'Emperor's New Clothes' thing, right? You want me to see something that's not really there."

"Heavens no," Ann replied. "We want you to see something that *is* there."

"You just won't see it until you look closer," Phil added.

Nick turned to the couple. "I looked in the mirror. I saw myself. How can I look closer than that?"

"Just focus," Ann explained.

"Focus? On what?"

"On your gifts, sweetie. Things that you can offer other people. That's why you're wearing a gift wrap suit."

"Focusing on my gifts is going to change what I see?"

Ann answered slowly so her words would sink in. "When you see yourself as others see you, your image of yourself will change."

Nick looked toward the mirrors, willing to try, but unsure how to begin. Sensing his uncertainty, Phil picked up a yardstick and ran a hand along its length.

"We should measure our success by what we give rather then what we have. Each of us has three gifts that we can share. There's a mirror to reflect each one."

He pointed the stick at the bronze plaques over the frames. Each was engraved with a single word. He tapped the words for emphasis as he spoke. "We can share our *Treasures*, our *Talents*, and our *Time*."

Phil pointed to the mirror on the left. "Let's start with *Treasures*. Are you generous with material things?"

Nick smirked playfully as if unimpressed with the fabric he was wearing. "I'm a little more generous with material than you two are." He searched their faces for a smile but found none. "I'm also a little more generous with the laughs."

Phil questioned him again. "Do you share what

you have with others?"

"I tip well," Nick explained, "but I can't say that I go out of my way in the charity department."

"Why not?"

"Force of habit, I guess. I don't really do anything unless I get something in return. It's just not good business."

"You didn't always feel that way."

"I can't remember when I didn't."

"That's what the mirror is for."

Phil pointed to the glass, and Nick was startled to see his reflection fade away. A new image filled the frame, foggy yet familiar, as if a memory were being projected onto the glass.

Nick saw himself as a teenager, roughly fourteen years old. He sat in the passenger seat of the family car, staring out the window. His mother sat beside him, humming along with a Christmas carol playing softly on the car stereo.

"I was in high school then. You had to go back pretty far to make your point."

"It's a pretty good point."

The car pulled into the parking lot of the local grocery store and came to rest beneath a light pole decorated for the winter holidays. As they climbed out and walked to the back of the car, a Salvation Army bell rang in the distance.

Nick watched as his mother opened the trunk. His younger self reached in and removed a large pickle jar filled to the brim with coins.

Nick smiled as he watched himself carrying the container toward the front of the store. "Our family money jar," he said to Phil. "We never spent the change we had in our pockets. We just tossed it into that old jar all year long. It always amazed me how full the thing got by December."

Nick looked back to the mirror as he and his mother approached the volunteer standing by the red bucket. Nick watched himself unscrew the lid and tilt the jar. As the coins on top trickled in, the volunteer's eyes began to widen. Nick's grin widened with them as he watched his younger self tilt the jar, sending the coins cascading into the bucket.

Nick laughed and pointed, "I love the look on

that guy's face."

Phil pointed, too, "I love the look on yours."

Nick shifted focus and was surprised by what he saw: the light in the younger Nick's eyes, the joy in his smile, the spirit in his step as he strolled away cradling the empty jar. He opened the door for his mother and blushed as she gave him a hug. The older Nick blushed as well.

"We never had a lot of money," he offered. "But we never missed a chance to surprise those volunteers."

"There are always people who are less fortunate than you, Nick. When you are blessed, you need to share your blessings."

The image on the mirror was suddenly covered by a stream of silver coins that fell within the glass. As they settled out of the frame, the image Nick had been watching was gone, replaced, once again, by his own reflection: a reflection clothed in the bright red paper jacket.

Nick touched the jacket on his chest and watched the reflection do the same. Glancing right, he saw that the jacket was visible only within the mirror marked

Treasures.

"Your family taught you the power of giving," Phil explained. "Again and again, you shared what you had with those who had less. You remember how that felt. The image in the glass reflects that."

"My turn! My turn!" Ann took Nick's shoulders and turned him toward the mirror in the middle. "Gift number two: your *Talents.*"

Nick looked at his center reflection and saw no jacket. Worse yet, he saw a man with no discernible talents.

"This is going to be a tough one," he said.

"Nonsense! Just think of something you're good at."

"I'm a good salesman, but that's about it. I don't participate in sports. I don't play a musical instrument. I'm drawing a blank."

"You drew more than that back in college."

Ann waved at the mirror. Nick's reflection vanished from top to bottom as if a giant eraser were rubbing against the glass; each stroke revealed a piece of a new image hidden underneath. It was an image of Nick in his early twenties, sitting at a drafting table, sketching with a pencil while a young woman roughly the same age looked over his shoulder.

"Amber Carson," Nick said, a smile of recognition flashing over his face. "Editor-in-chief of the college newspaper."

"You worked for her?"

"I worshiped her. She caught me sketching her in economics class and asked me to join the staff. I contributed the occasional political cartoon."

"Were they any good?"

"Amber thought so. Most people did, I guess."

"Why'd you stop drawing? Didn't you think you had talent?"

"My drawings were clever, but I was realistic. I didn't think my art was going to change the world."

"Think again."

Ann waved at the mirror. The image of Nick and Amber ripped away like a page being torn from a sketchpad. A new image appeared. Nick, still college-age, was sitting at a kitchen table. A young man stood behind him, his face buried in the refrigerator.

Nick looked closely, then shook his head. "I have

no idea where this is." The refrigerator closed, revealing a familiar face. "That's Randy Neff."

"And who was he?"

"My roommate, junior year. We must be at his house. He went home every few weeks for a home-cooked meal. I went along a few times. What does this have to do with art?"

Ann nodded toward the mirror. A young boy about twelve years old walked into the kitchen and set a stack of spiral notebooks on the table. Randy rolled his eyes and wandered out of the room.

"Who's he?" Nick asked.

"Jeremy Neff. Randy's little brother."

"I don't remember him."

"Well, you inspired him."

Nick saw himself looking through the spiral notebooks. A fragment of a memory returned. "He showed me homemade comic books or something. They were pretty good for a kid."

"You were the first one to tell him that. The first one to take his drawings seriously. You showed him quite a few tips, too."

Nick nodded, remembering more. "I brought him an old set of my pencils the next time I visited. We sketched his whole family while they watched some football game on TV."

"He still has those sketches in his studio."

"He's an artist?"

"An art teacher. You encouraged him. Now, he encourages others. Do you know the mural on the back wall of the library?"

"The characters stepping out of the books? My daughter loved that when she was little."

"One of his students did that. Another one just opened an art school for underprivileged kids. All of Mr. Neff's students take a piece of him with them. In a way, they take a piece of you, too."

The image of Nick and Jeremy began to run from the mirror like wet paint dripping down a canvas. Nick saw his reflection return to the center glass. The coat of red wrapping paper was in place as he had hoped.

"You shared a talent that continues to affect lives," Ann said, admiring the reflection. "Seek out new talents to share and you'll enrich other lives. None more than your own."

She moved to her husband's side. Nick turned to the final mirror and looked at his reflection. "This guy needs a coat!" he called out, eager to get started. "It's time for *Time*. Which one of you is going to take me through this one?"

Max set down his magazine and stood. "I'll take this one, if the two of you don't mind. I promise to make it quick."

Phil stepped aside. "By all means, take your time."

Ann moved as well. "No one knows time better than you."

Nick felt nervous watching Max approach. His powers still made him a foreboding presence. Max gestured to the mirror on the right.

"Let's see how generous you are with your time, Nick."

Nick stood facing the mirror. Though he stayed perfectly still, his reflection turned sideways and hugged a little girl who wandered into the image. Dressed in pink pajamas, she placed her feet upon his and grabbed both of his hands to keep her balance.

"That's my daughter, Grace. We used to waltz every night before bed."

"How old is she there?"

"Five. Maybe six."

"She's pretty."

"She takes after her mother."

Alicia entered the picture, applauding as Nick and Grace held hands and bowed.

"Here comes our big finish," Nick bragged. "I called it the Tango Tuck-In."

Alicia lifted Grace and placed her into Nick's arms. Putting his cheek against his daughter's, Nick stretched her arm out with his and pranced her down the hallway. When he reached the end, he dipped her, kissed her while she giggled, and disappeared into a doorway. Alicia followed, closing the door to reveal a pink-painted sign reading, "Grace's Room."

Nick turned to Max. "I haven't thought about those dances for years."

"Grace has."

"She's twelve now," Nick said, sounding more

defensive than he meant to. "She doesn't want to dance with me anymore."

"She wants to dance *for* you."

Nick returned his attention to the mirror. The sign reading "Grace's Room" dissolved into one reading, "Green Room." It opened slowly, revealing a room bursting with excitement. A parade of young dancers, glowing after a just-finished performance, were finding their way into the embraces of proud parents.

In the flash of cameras, Nick saw Grace searching for someone to help her celebrate. Seeing her run into Alicia's arms, Nick noted his daughter's eyes darting around the room. He watched Alicia hand Grace a bouquet of flowers and saw Grace's smile fade as she read the card. Nick looked down, his eyes beginning to water.

"I sent the flowers because I got stuck at work. Grace said she understood."

"What did you expect her to say?"

Nick stood in silence, unable to respond.

"There'll be other performances, Nick," Max lifted

Nick's head toward the mirror. Grace was dancing alone on a stage.

"I'll make time for the next one," Nick said, speaking directly to Grace. "I promise."

"Your presence is the greatest present you can give." Max stepped back, leaving Nick alone to watch. "Time is a precious gift," he explained, "impossible to replace once it is lost. Share it with those who will appreciate it the most."

Grace finished her dance with a flourish then curtsied as the stage lights began to fade. The blackness lingered for a moment then parted slowly to reveal Nick's reflection, the red paper jacket visible to all.

Phil stepped up to Nick's side. "You look great, kid. Generosity suits you well."

Ann moved to his other side. "You're a gift, Nick. Can you see that now?"

Nick checked his reflection in all three mirrors. He ran his hands along the lapel of the paper jacket. "I'm ... a ... gift. A gift. All I need now is a *bow* tie!" He pointed to the collar. "Gift? Bow? Come on. That one's funny!"

There was a beat of silence followed by a quick burst of laughter from everyone in the room. Phil placed a hand on Nick's shoulder. Ann leaned over and touched Nick's forearm. Max reached forward and patted his back. Nick sighed and smiled ... until he heard the rips.

They came suddenly and simultaneously from all sides. Crisp, clean, and quick. Max, Phil, and Ann tore the paper like eager children at Christmastime. The jacket was off his body and onto the floor before he could even speak.

Nick collected his thoughts while the others bent to pick up the pieces.

"Why did you do that?"

Ann looked up, "We wrapped up the lesson ... "

Phil stood and finished the response. " ... by unwrapping the ultimate gift."

Nick sighed as they placed the scraps into a trash can. "I liked it. I thought I was going to get to keep it."

Max shook his head. "You don't need it." He turned Nick to the mirror and pointed to the reflection. "It's always there." Nick concentrated and saw the wrapping paper re-appear in the magic mirrors. "You've been a gift your whole life. You'd just forgotten how it felt."

A bell rang out from across the shop as if to signal the arrival of a customer. Nick spun toward the sound and watched the front door swing wide open.

Nick watched in anticipation, then shrugged. "The door opened, but no one came in."

Max gestured to the door. "I guess that means we're supposed to go."

Ann gave Max a hug good-bye. Phil shook his hand, then turned to Nick. "Here, take this."

"A business card?"

"Our gift to you. Chime Three reminds you of the three things to give others: your treasures, your talent, and your time. Everything that you have and are is a gift to you. What you make of it is your gift back."

Nick looked at the card. The third chime was written on the back. He took out his watch and read.

⇒ CHIME 3 ⇐

TIME TO GIVE

I give of my time to help others.

I give of my talents to aid someone or something beyond my work.

I give of my treasure and share my material things with others.

I measure success by what I give rather than what I have.

Nick held the card out toward Max. "Trade ya."

Max took the card and slid it into a pocket. Another number appeared on Nick's watch.

Nick grabbed his jacket from the hanger. He turned toward Phil and Ann and thanked them for their help.

"You're welcome," Ann said, gesturing to the door. "Let us show you out."

Nick stepped through the doorway and discovered that the tailor shop was the corner store in a row of small businesses. He was wondering whether they would head left or right when he glanced across the street. A vast landscape towered before him, a forest in the midst of the city. Tree branches waved in the breeze, beckoning him.

MOSAIC PARK

MAX AND NICK STROLLED TOWARD THE EDGE OF THE wooded park. A thin path of stones ran diagonally through the tapestry of brown and green. As they wandered into the thicket, the path widened beneath their feet.

"Let me guess this one," Nick said. "Time for Nature ... Time for the Outdoors ... "

"Time to be quiet."

"There's no one here. Who am I disturbing?"

"You're disturbing me."

"Oh, sorry." Nick walked in silence until he was overcome with curiosity. "Can you just tell me why we're in a forest?"

"I don't see a forest."

Nick looked at the trunks rising on both sides of the walkway. "Okay. If this is a 'can't see the forest for the trees' thing, I'm confused."

Max stopped. "I can't see a forest because we're not in one."

Nick pointed to his surroundings. "We're walking through the middle of a bunch of trees."

"We're walking through the middle of one tree." Max reached up and touched a leaf. "This is an aspen, Nick. Everything you see branches off of a single root system. Things in life are often connected in unexpected ways."

"So, we're here to learn about connections?"

"We're here to learn about relationships."

They continued along the stone path and around a small bend. Nick was amazed by the majesty of the single tree that surrounded them.

"Relationships are all interconnected," Max

explained. "Choose to respect them, nurture them, help them grow."

Nick stopped and leaned against a large tree. With a delicate trunk and arching limbs, it was obviously different from the other.

"This isn't part of the aspen," Nick said. "What is this?"

"A willow," Max explained. "A weeping willow, to be exact."

"Are you sure? It doesn't look like it's weeping."

"It's weeping. Perhaps you're unfamiliar with the concept?"

"Weeping? I weep. Sometimes. I guess."

"When was the last time you cried?"

Nick was surprised by the slowness of his own response. His mind dug deep until it struck water. "I cried ... at my grandfather's funeral."

"Why?"

"Because I loved him and I lost him."

"Tell me about him."

Nick shook his head. He had replayed the memories in the clock shop. He wasn't about to relive them again. "I already did."

"You only told me he left you his watch when he died. I want to know about his life." Max sat with his back to the tree. "Tell me one story. Something he did that made you smile."

Nick sighed at the old man's persistence. He searched his memory for a lighthearted moment, his face glowing slightly as he found it. "There was a magic trick he used to do at family gatherings. We'd be celebrating a holiday, having a big dinner, going to a church service ... and I'd notice my grandfather looking at me from across the room. He'd start squinting his eyes and scrunching his face like he noticed something weird."

Nick caught himself imitating his grandfather's expression. He continued the story, acting it out as he remembered it.

"He'd walk over to where I was, fix my hair, straighten my tie, wipe a smudge from my cheek... but he'd keep staring like there was still something wrong. Finally, his eyes would go wide and he'd get this big smile on his face. He'd open his hand, reach up to my ear, and pull out a silver dollar."

Nick paused in mid-pantomime. He could almost see the coin in his fingertips.

Max wanted more. "What would he do then?"

"He'd place it in my palm and close my fingers around it. Said the same thing to me every time, too." Nick's throat began to tighten. He used the emotion to mimic his grandfather's voice. "Spend it wisely, Nicholas. Spend it wisely."

He closed his eyes to hold back the tears. He offered a silent prayer for his grandfather and passed the imaginary coin into an unseen hand. He was surprised by the sound of metal striking stone.

Opening his eyes, he saw Max pick something up from the path. Max rose to his feet and revealed a golden coin.

Nick eyed it with uncertainty. "Where'd you get that?"

"You dropped it."

"I wasn't holding anything."

"You were holding a memory," Max replied. "A memento of the past, as solid and precious as gold."

He held the coin for Nick to see. "Your grandfather may have given you money, but he was sharing something more valuable. He was sharing time." Max placed the coin into Nick's hands. "Hold on to the memory, and he'll always be with you."

Nick considered Max's words, then smiled. He passed the coin from one hand to the other and squeezed it tightly. Unfurling his fingers one by one, he revealed the hand to be empty.

"He's gone," Nick said, "but he's still here." He reached up to Max's ear and came back with the coin in his fingertips.

Max smiled at the trick. "Your grandfather invested his time wisely. He extended his life experience. He lives on in you … "

" … like magic." Nick slipped the coin into his pocket so it nestled against his watch. "I really do feel him with me sometimes."

"There are others with you, too," Max said. "You may not feel them as strongly, but they are there." He gestured forward and began to walk. "Think of your life as a path, Nick: A journey from one point to another. Every stone you pass can be seen as a relationship you encounter along the way."

Nick studied the path, suddenly aware of the variation in the stones. Max pointed to several as he spoke. "Some are smooth," he explained. "Some jagged. Others fragile."

Each of the examples triggered a memory in Nick's mind: the laughter of a lifelong friend, a quarrel with a co-worker, a broken deal with a potential client.

He stopped suddenly next to a large, flat rock. A deep crack bent like a shark fin across its surface, nearly splitting it in two. The shape of the fracture and severity of the break provoked a series of painful images: His father packing. His mother crying. A twelve-year-old boy torn between sorrow and hate.

Nick kicked the rock and moved on. "Some of them," he sighed, "are beyond repair." He had walked a few feet when he felt Max's hand on his shoulder.

"We all have broken stones on our path, Nick. We can choose to mend them or we can choose to live with them the way they are. Either way, they are a part of us. All the stones are. From the smallest to the most monumental, each one adds dimension and color."

Max led Nick through a clearing in the trees. Although the path continued, it widened suddenly, expanding into a massive mosaic design. The stones, a stunning array of size, shape, and shade, sprawled outward into a vast courtyard. Businessmen laughed as they lunched near a food cart. A giggling baby girl holding a helium balloon rode high on her father's shoulders. A stout, jovial woman with an instant camera snapped pictures of a couple posing with a poodle.

"What is this place?"

"It's the town square."

Nick smiled as he surveyed the surroundings. "It doesn't look square." He pointed to an oval area to his left. "I'd say some of it is even round."

"The trees form a perfect square. The paths come in from the four corners." Max pointed to the distance. "You can see the whole thing from an old church tower just beyond those trees."

Nick looked toward the center of the courtyard. The woman with the camera was now taking photographs of a laughing family. Behind her, Nick noticed several workers in white overalls diligently adjusting the stones.

"Who are they?"

"Artisans. It's their job to assemble the design."

Nick watched them closely. Two of the workers were lifting heavy stones and swapping their positions. Another was chiseling away at a jagged rock. A fourth was holding pieces, polishing them to a brilliant luster.

"What are they doing?"

"Rearranging. Redefining. Refinishing. Putting them in proper perspective. Each stone has a special place, Nick. Be aware of which ones need tending to ... which ones are most important to the grand design."

"It's not finished?"

"It's like life, Nick. It's always evolving."

"And evolving beautifully!" The woman with the camera wandered up to them. "Been staring at it all morning. Simply fascinating!" She extended a hand.

"Rhonda Johnson, town square photographer."

Nick and Max shared a quizzical look.

"Didn't mean to eavesdrop on your conversation. I heard the two of you discussing the design and I thought I ... " She paused for a moment and squinted at Nick's face. "Have we met before?"

"I don't believe so. I'm not from around here."

"Funny. You look familiar. I swear I've seen you someplace." She stared for another second, shook her head, and shrugged. "Anyway! You ready for your picture?"

"Our picture?"

"Free photo for everyone who visits the square!" She peered through her camera and waved the two men closer together. "Side by side. That's right. Act like you like each other. Perfect! Smile, gents."

A button clicked, the camera whirred, and a photograph slid out. Rhonda presented it to Max. "It'll take a few minutes, but it's gonna turn out great. Only one per party, though. You and your friend will get to decide who keeps it."

She bid them good-bye and headed off.

Nick raised his eyebrow. "She was interesting."

Max smiled and moved away. "Another colorful stone in the path of your life."

Nick leaned to get a glimpse of the photo, but Max managed to keep it out of view. "You'd be in that path, too, wouldn't you be Max?"

"I suppose I would. And you'd be in mine. The photographer did refer to us as friends."

"Is that what we have now? A friendship?"

"We'll have to see," Max said, slipping the photo into a pocket. "At this point, it's still developing."

Max winked, walked to the oval area of the courtyard and stopped near a small pool. A young couple who had been sitting there strolled off hand in hand toward an identical pool a few feet away. Nick watched them leave, leaned in, and looked over the edge. Clear water glimmered in a circle of white stone. A large, smooth sapphire sat in the center, painting the bottom a brilliant blue.

"Are these wishing fountains?"

"They could be, I guess. I always considered them reflection ponds myself." Max noticed a glimmer in Nick's eye. "Looks like you're reflecting on something already."

Nick blushed a bit. "Reminiscing, really. I made a wish in a fountain like this once. With Alicia. One of our first dates."

"Sounds romantic."

"It was." Nick paused as the evening replayed, flickering through his mind like a reel from a Hollywood movie. Alicia's head on his shoulder as they strolled through the park … the street lamp that dimmed, granting a private kiss … the fountain they happened upon and the pennies they tossed in it.

"What did you wish for?"

"I wished that the two us would fall in love."

"And?"

"And … it came true. We're together. We're married. We're … "

"Happy?"

Nick stopped in mid-thought. He tested several answers in his head, before choosing one he was comfortable with. He turned away as he said it aloud.

"Mostly."

Max jumped in front of him, posing as if reading

from a book. "And they lived happily ever after ... mostly." He shrugged. "Not quite the story you were hoping for, is it?"

"So we have a few problems. A few cracks in the stone. It's nothing I can't fix."

Max nodded and headed for the center of the courtyard. "Choose to know which ones need tending to," he muttered, "which ones are most important to the grand design."

Max walked away. Nick lowered his head, shoved his hands in his pockets, and shuffled after him. He'd taken only a few steps when his hand came out holding the gold coin. Staring at it silently for a moment, he turned and headed for the second fountain. He tossed the coin toward the water.

"I wish that the two of us would fall in love ... again."

As the coin sank into the water, Nick's spirits rose in anticipation of a rekindled romance. He knew it would take more than a wish to mend the rifts, but he was ready to begin again, to win his wife's heart the same way he had done some twenty years before.

Turning and heading after Max, Nick hurried past the center of the courtyard. He caught up to him at the opposite end of the park.

"Are we through here?"

"One more stop," said Max. "Right at the end of the path."

They walked in silence for several moments. The path thinned out as it passed through the trees, coming to an end on a city street. Max pointed to his right. "There it is," he said. "The old church."

"We can see the whole square from the tower, right?"

"We can if we climb to the top."

They wandered along the road until they reached the church. It was a simple wood building with stained glass windows and a large oak door that stood wide open. Nick leaned in and looked. A few people, scattered in the pews, sat silently in prayer.

"I haven't been to a service since I was a kid," Nick whispered. "It's been a long time since I was even in a church."

"When was the last time?"

Nick paused to think. "My grandfather's funeral."

"And before that?"

He paused again. "My daughter's christening."

"Before that?"

He sighed. "My wedding … "

"If your deepest relationships keep bringing you to church, why not reconnect with your spirituality and strengthen those relationships even more?"

Nick sighed. "My family has such a strong faith. I'm afraid mine waivers a bit."

"No need to be afraid. Nobody's faith starts out strong. You have to use it to strengthen it. Plant a seed of faith in your heart. Your heart is fertile ground. With strong faith, all of your relationships will grow." Max led Nick gently from the door. "You can come back any time you want."

They moved across the church toward the base of the steeple. They entered an opening in the square base and climbed a stairway all the way to the top. Stepping out on the balcony, Nick looked out over the trees, getting a clear view of the town square.

The intricate mosaic revealed an unexpected

image. Stretching below him in grand scale was the body of a man. The eyes, two pools of shimmering blue, gleamed upward as if looking at Nick. The arms, paths of stone bending through the brush, extended wide as if welcoming a friend.

"I don't believe it," he whispered, recapturing his breath. "It's ... me."

Nick stared in astonishment at the accuracy of the design. The arrangement of trees outlined the figure, creating the shape of his body. The shading of the stones perfectly rendered his features, from the hint of gray in his thinning hair to polished scuffs on his well-traveled shoes.

Max placed his hands on Nick's shoulder. "Things connect in unexpected ways, Nick. The people we let in our lives become a part of us. They give shape to our life. They define who we are."

A sudden ringing of church bells rattled the tower and sent nesting pigeons scattering into flight. Startled by the sound, Nick grabbed a railing and waited for the vibrations to pass. As the chimes faded, Max patted his pockets and removed an object. It was the photograph the woman had taken in the square.

Max handed the picture to Nick. "Chime Four reminds you of the four relationships to cherish and kindle. Your creator, your family, your friends, and your fellow man." Nick looked at the image of him and Max, smiling brightly, a friendship fully developed. Beneath the photo, in perfect script, was the Fourth Chime.

⊷ CHIME 4 ⊶

TIME FOR RELATIONSHIPS

I love who I am.

I invest quality time in the relationships that are important to me.

I develop my spirituality.

I approach everyone I meet with love in my heart.

Nick handed the photo back. Max smiled at the image then dropped it into an inside pocket. Nick removed his watch and saw the number four appear slowly into place.

"Four numbers," Nick explained, holding the watch out for Max to see. "I'm a third of the way there."

"We've still got a ways to go," Max said, turning and heading down the stairs. "Let's get going or we're going to miss the boat!"

The Sea of Knowledge

Nick followed Max from the balcony of the church onto the tower stairs. He was moving down the steps when it occurred to him that the shape of the stairwell was shifting. The square walls of the tower were rounding off as he descended. The right angles of the stairway were gradually turning into spirals.

Nick called ahead for an explanation. Max paused and pointed to a doorway at the bottom of the final flight. "Open her up."

Nick slipped past Max and proceeded down the steps. He pushed through the door and felt a sudden rush to his senses: the smell and taste of a salty breeze, the warmth of sunlight reflected off the sand, the sight and sound of waves on rock.

"How'd we get to the beach?"

Nick turned to look back at Max and was surprised to see the whole town was gone. The church tower was now a lighthouse and the surroundings, a rustic seaside landscape. Max stepped though the doorway, squinted into the sun, and scanned the shore.

Nick mimicked his actions. "Are you looking for something in particular?"

"Not something. *Someone*. And he's *very* particular."

Nick looked to the beach. He saw rolling waves, jagged rocks, and little else. He tapped Max on the shoulder.

"You expect to find your friend out there?"

"Not with you distracting me." Max chuckled and looked back to the coastline. "His name's Ken. He's a retired sea captain. He keeps the lighthouse."

Nick pointed behind him. "Wouldn't he be up

there, then?"

"He would be if he weren't on break." Max smiled as he spotted something in the distance. "There he is now."

Nick stared until he saw what Max did. A black man in a blue sailor's cap reclined on a jetty unaffected by the waves that crashed around him. His body rested against the rocks as if they were the softest of pillows. His face was buried in a book.

Max looked from the sun to the sea. He gauged the time by shadows cast by rocks. "He's a stickler for schedules. He should be finished any moment."

As if on cue, Ken closed the book and rose to his feet. He took a deep breath of the cool sea air and turned toward the lighthouse. He raised his hand excitedly as he spotted Max, then hurried along the rocks.

Max leaned to Nick as the captain approached. "I have to warn you about Ken's language."

"Pretty salty?"

"Peppered, actually."

"Peppered?"

"With famous quotations, historical references, literary allusions. The man's a voracious reader."

Ken shouted as he grew nearer. "Well, call me Ishmael! If it's not my old friend, Max!" He stuck his book under his arm and shook Max's hand. "It's been too long!"

"Sure has," Max said. "I see you're reading as usual."

Ken raised a finger and recited a quote. "'There is no friend as loyal as a book.'" He cupped his hand to his mouth as he credited the author. "Ernest Hemingway."

"Captain Ken, I'd like you to meet Nick."

Nick shook Ken's hand, pointing to the book under his arm.

"So, what are you reading?"

Ken laughed as he held it up. "Hemingway, again. *The Old Man and the Sea*. I was so busy living it, I never got around to reading it. Figured I better dive in and find out what I'd missed. Never stop feeding the noggin, you know." He tapped the book against the side of his cap. "So, what brings the two of you here?"

"We need someone to bring the two of us *there*."

Max pointed to the horizon. The outline of an island floated in the distance like a shadow bobbing on the sea.

"I know just the man," Ken smiled. "And he just happens to be my boy!"

He pointed through a patch of cattails. A burly young man stood on a small dock polishing the sides of a sailboat.

Max looked surprised. "That can't be your son, Kip?"

"It can and is."

"I haven't seen him in years. He's older than I recall."

"Older and wiser. You remember why I called him Kip, don't you?"

Max nodded. "K-I-P. Knowledge is Power."

Ken beamed and led the men toward the dock. "There was never a boy more aptly named. An explorer. A teacher. A thinker. He's fashioned himself into one of the finest sailors I've ever seen. Strong in muscle but stronger in mind."

They reached the dock and called for Kip. A

broad-shouldered man in his mid-thirties, he greeted them warmly, agreeing without hesitation to take them on their journey. He smiled proudly as he presented his ship. *"The Stallion II. She's ready when you are."*

"We're ready now," said Max. "If it won't be a bother?"

"It'll be my pleasure." Kip gestured for the men to step aboard. "Every journey is an opportunity for adventure ... an invitation to experience something different ... a chance to learn something new." He raised a finger and recited a quote in the same manner as his father. "'Thought is the wind, knowledge the sail, and mankind the vessel.'" He cupped his hand to his mouth. "Augustus Hare."

Ken patted his son on the back. "That's my boy!" He gave Kip a solid hug and watched him board the ship. "Enjoy the voyage, gentlemen. You're in good hands."

"You should be," Kip said. "Dad taught me everything he knows."

"No, I taught you everything *you* know." Ken

grinned and tapped his book on the side of his cap. "I've still got a few gems tucked away." He gave a wave as he turned, opened the pages, and began reading as he strolled up the dock.

Nick looked on as Kip watched his father walk away. Max watched Nick, sensing a hint of melancholy in his friend.

He distracted Nick with a question. "Ready for your sailing lesson?"

"Lesson? I thought we were taking a trip to the island."

"Well, you can't get anywhere unless you know a little about navigation."

"Let's start with *The Five Ds*," said Kip. "The first D: *Desire*. You've got to have it. The entire journey is powered by it. Your desire to grow ... your desire to learn ... your desire to get the most out of life."

Kip took a wrinkled map from his jacket pocket and tossed it to Nick.

"What's this for?"

"The second D: *Discovery*. Before you can focus on where you want to go, you must first discover where you are."

Nick responded without unfolding the map. "I'm not going to be able to read this. I have no idea where we are."

Max pulled it open for him and pointed to a sketch of a shoreline with a large lighthouse. He dragged his finger to a rendering of a boat with a large arrow drawn above it. He pointed to the words in bold print: You Are Here.

Nick smiled sheepishly. "Got it. What's next?"

"The third D: *Destination*," Kip replied. "Know where you want to go." He raised a finger and recited a line to illustrate his point. "'*Ignoranti, quem portum petat, nullus suus ventus est.*' Seneca, Roman philosopher. 'If one does not know to which port one is sailing, no wind is favorable.'"

Nick nodded and looked to the sea. He located the island he had seen earlier and pointed. "We're headed there."

"Time for the fourth D then: *Direction*. How do we get where we want to be?"

Nick lifted the map and aligned it with the image

on the horizon. "Due north?"

"North it is!" Max said. He shouted as he pointed forward. "Let's go!"

Kip cheered, matching Max's enthusiasm. "That's the fifth D! *Determination*! Commitment! Focus! Action!"

There was a flurry of movement. Line released, levers shifted, and sails unfurled. In a matter of minutes, *The Stallion II* captured the wind and sailed out onto the open sea.

Nick marveled at the precision of Kip's actions. "That was fast."

Kip smiled and settled in behind the wheel. "Got it down to a science. It used to take me twenty minutes to launch this baby. Felt like I was wasting time, so I developed a system. Saves me fifteen minutes every time I leave port."

"Impressive."

"Five trips a day. That's over an extra hour of time. More time to get things done. More time to relax. More time to enjoy the journey."

Nick placed the map in his pocket and leaned

back to take in the surroundings. Sunlight glistened warmly off the crystal blue water. Sea gulls soared overhead.

"It's beautiful out here."

"A feast for the five senses," Kip explained. "A Sea of Knowledge, if you will. Vast, deep, endlessly enlightening."

"Is it always this peaceful?"

"It's unpredictable, really. There are moments of smooth sailing, when the wind is in your sail and the current is with you. But there are unexpected storms on nearly every journey. You have to pay attention at all times. Learn from the things you encounter." He glanced around. "I can tell you right now that there's a shark nearby."

"How do you know?"

Kip pointed portside. "Something I learned from the school of fish."

Nick leaned and looked down. Beneath the surface, barely visible, was a large group of fish. They cut through the water in a single direction until they disappeared beneath the boat. A shadowy form with a dorsal fin glided after them.

Nick turned, impressed by Kip's powers of observation. "How'd you know that was happening?"

"Experience. Observation. You have to be pretty quick to see a shark. They don't stay around for long."

Nick nodded. "They have to keep moving or they'll die."

"Why do you say that?'

"Just something I heard when I was a kid."

Kip shrugged. "That's just a piece of sailor's lore. I'm afraid whoever told you that was mistaken."

Nick was taken aback by what he heard. He turned and sat as thoughts of his father resurfaced. Max spoke.

"Sometimes the things we think we know turn out to be wrong."

"What do you mean?"

"There are things you believe that just aren't so. Information you've misunderstood, assumptions you've accepted as fact, or ideas about your own limitations. Choose to discover for yourself how good you can be, how much you can do, how far you can go. Have you ever heard of the coelacanth?"

Nick shook his head. Max sat beside him and explained.

"The coelacanth is a fish that pre-dated the dinosaurs. It was believed to have been extinct for 65 million years. In 1938, someone pulled a live one out of a fishing net and everything changed. A moment of discovery can restructure our beliefs. The key is to be open-minded."

Max stood and called to Kip. "Speaking of moments, what do you say we take a few and do a little fishing?"

Kip turned the wheel to slow the boat. Max moved to the mast to lower the sail. Nick stood, ready to learn something new.

"I've never fished before. The two of you may have to show me a few things."

"Nick, my boy," Max smiled, "there's nothing we'd enjoy more."

The Stallion II settled down and the men settled in. There were lessons of leaders and lures, demonstrations of double knots, and revelations as to the origin of

Max's passion.

"Kip's father was the one who taught me to fish," Max explained. "It was my first trip to the island. He was so excited about showing me the ropes. I've been hooked ever since."

Kip laughed. "My father did the same with me. And not just with fishing. He shared his fascination for everything. For sailing, for reading. I pass on the same enthusiasm to others as well."

"That's one of the joys of learning, Nick. Sharing your excitement. Spreading your knowledge. Watching your lessons live on in your students."

Nick raised a finger and recited a quote. "'Give a man a fish and he eats for a day. Teach a man to fish and he eats for a lifetime.'"

"Catch a man a fish and he'll know you were paying attention," Max said as he waited for Nick to cast a line, then nodded his approval. "We're fishing for fun, anyway, not for food. We're just going to pull them out and throw them back."

"Then lie about the size!" Kip piped in.

Kip reeled in his line, removed a tuna, then

tossed it back into the sea. He held his hands out completely overestimating the size. "Did you see that one? She was a whopper!"

Max laughed, pulling up a flounder and flinging it back. "Mine was a five footer," he said. "And I measure mine between the eyes."

There was a bit of laughter and another bite on a line. Nick's pole arched like a rainbow.

"You've got one!" Max yelled. "A big one! Pull her in!"

Nick leapt to his feet, his heart pounding, his hands reeling, his mind spinning. With the instruction and encouragement of his two companions, he hauled a sizable grouper onto the deck. He laughed triumphantly, lifted his trophy, and tossed it back to the sea.

"Did you see that thing?" he exclaimed. "I'd say she was a twenty pounder!"

Max smiled proudly. "I'm glad we were here to witness it."

"If you hadn't been here, I'd say she was a *thirty* pounder!"

They laughed again, each preparing to make another cast, when they were interrupted by an unexpected change in the weather.

An enormous dark cloud appeared in the sky before them. There was an intense crash of thunder, then waves broke the stillness of the sea. A second cloud appeared an instant later and a thunderclap sent the men scurrying for their seats. Three more clouds arrived in quick succession, enveloping the boat like a ring of black mountains rising from the depths.

Waves began thrashing against the ship, tossing it in several directions. Water crashed over the sides, splashing onto the deck. Nick called to Kip, his shaky voice nearly lost in the rising winds.

"Is the storm going to be as bad as it looks?"

"No," Kip replied. "It's going to be worse."

A bolt of lightning flashed like an exclamation point. A burst of thunder heralded a sudden downpour.

Trapped in swirling winds, surging waves, and pouring rain, Nick felt himself being pelted from every direction. *The Stallion II* tipped, taking in more water. Max lost his balance, slipped, and fell hard to the deck. His locket flew out from under his collar, crashing against the surface. Nick bent and helped Max up, his heart sinking as he saw the fear in the old man's face.

"Are we going to be all right?"

Max stood, tucking the locket back into his shirt. "I'm ... I'm not sure."

"Well, I am!"

It was Kip. He thrust two life jackets into their hands and led them toward the center of the ship. "We're all going to be all right, but I'm going to need your help."

They moved through the rising water and gathered around the mast. When the men had fastened their life jackets, Kip snatched the line that lifted the sail and placed it in their hands. "Wait for my signal, then pull. Hard."

They watched through the rain as Kip returned to the helm of *The Stallion II*. He rode the waves like a cowboy breaking a wild horse: one hand steady on the wheel, the other raised high in the air. He maneuvered through wind and water, avoiding devastation by the thinnest of margins. It was in a slight lull between crashing waves that he finally gave the word.

"NOW!"

The men pulled the line and the sail snapped to life, rocketing through the gathering water like a phoenix bursting from the flames. It ascended skyward, widening as it rose, reaching its full height and width in a swift and powerful motion. The sail caught the storm like wings capturing wind, and *The Stallion II* propelled upward. She scaled the wall of the mounting wave, gaining height and speed until she vaulted from the peak.

In an instant, she was airborne.

Kip bellowed from behind the wheel. *The Stallion II* soared above the torrent, tilting slightly to shed herself of the unwanted water. She broke through a black cloud, spending a few glorious seconds in flight before splashing down safely in the crystal clear water outside of the storm.

Kip straightened the ship and headed for the island. He called out to his crew. "Perfect timing, men! Excellent work. Couldn't have done it without you."

Nick caught his breath. "How did you know you could do it at all?"

"I didn't. I just improvised. I took what I knew about wind and water and went for it."

Max removed a handkerchief from a coat pocket and began patting his face dry. "It was a nice call, Kip. Your father will be impressed. I've never been in a storm like that in my life."

"I have," Kip grimaced. "Once, anyway."

"You have?" Nick asked. "How'd you get your ship through the first one?"

"I didn't. Why do you think we're on *The Stallion II*?" He steered the boat into the island dock, sighing as he pointed to the sea. "*The Stallion I* is out there … somewhere. I thought I could steer her through on my own. Today, when I needed help, I asked for it. Lucky for me, I learn from my mistakes."

Nick smiled. "Lucky for all of us."

Kip rang the ship's bell, officially announcing their arrival. "Chime Five reminds you to learn with your five senses. Acquire knowledge to navigate your journey. Teach what you know and learn something new everyday." He pointed to the map in Nick's pocket. "Take a look at the back," he said. "My father wrote something for you."

Nick reached for his watch, looked at the map, and read.

⟢ CHIME 5 ⟣

TIME TO LEARN

I seek knowledge to better myself.

I learn from my experiences and rarely repeat mistakes.

I learn, implement and improve systems to make the most of my time.

I teach what I know to help others.

Nick stared at his watch for a few moments as the number five appeared. He showed it to Kip and followed Max off of the boat.

Kip steered back toward open waters. "Hope you enjoyed the journey," he called. "It turned out to be an adventure after all!"

The ship caught a breeze and began moving out to sea. Kip tapped the side of his head and shouted as he waved good-bye. "'Live as if you're going to die tomorrow. Learn as if you will live forever.' Gandhi. It's your knowledge that will navigate your life. Never stop feeding the noggin!"

The men waved from the edge of the dock as they watched the ship sail into the distance.

"We won't stop feeding the noggin," Max said. "But it's high time we start feeding the belly."

SOMEDAY

NICK FOLLOWED MAX DOWN THE LONG, WOODEN DOCK.

"We didn't come all this way for a meal, did we?"

"Of course not. That would be silly. It's more like a snack."

"A snack. What kind of snack?"

"All in good time, my boy. All in good time."

A wide, rectangular building stood in front of them. Max knocked on a large, metal door. An irritated man in a blue jumpsuit labeled "foreman" slid open the door and shuffled out. He consulted a clipboard and spoke.

"Delivery or pick-up?"

"Neither," Max shrugged. "Just passing through."

The foreman groaned and led them into a warehouse bustling with workers. The foreman pointed to a distant doorway. "Go straight through and stay out of the way. And make it snappy. We're a little swamped."

The foreman turned to avoid a rolling cart of books. Nick turned to Max.

"You want to get a snack in a warehouse?"

"I want to get a treat in the little town on the other side of the warehouse. That's why we're just passing through."

Max headed for a door in the distance. Nick followed for a few steps, then slowed down, distracted by what he saw. There were no boxes, as one would expect, just large piles of loose items. There were roses to his right, single stems, stacked high to the ceiling. There were envelopes to his left, stamped, addressed, and placed in tall piles. Ahead of him, blocking the path, was a massive, muscle-bound worker stacking exercise equipment onto a dangerously unstable mound.

Nick called ahead to Max. "What is all this?"

The foreman stepped between them and answered gruffly. "It's stuff that has to be done. And right now, you're in the way." He moved to a pile of postcards, rifled through them, and began listing the destinations they depicted.

"Where's all this stuff going?"

"Nowhere, yet. It all stays here until delivery day."

There was a sudden crash as the pile of exercise equipment toppled in the distance. The foreman slammed his clipboard on a countertop and stormed away. "Stack it again, Gunther! Carefully this time!"

Nick moved next to Max, keeping his eyes on the action surrounding him. Huge trucks backed through open doors, weary workers unloaded crate after crate, and stacks of materials grew more perilous with each passing moment.

"This place is chaotic."

"And this is a *slow* day." Max pointed to the clipboard at Nick's side. "Check the invoice. See when the delivery day is. It should be written right on the top."

Nick gave the clipboard a quick glance. "Everything's set to be delivered on ... Someday." He raised an eyebrow and turned to Max. "That's a mistake, right?"

"I'd say so."

"They probably meant 'Sunday.'"

"No. They meant 'Someday.'"

"But you said it was a mistake?"

"It *is* a mistake. Look at these people. Setting everything aside to deal with later. They just don't get it." He pointed in the distance. "Look at that. They never even finished their sign."

Nick looked and saw a billboard propped against a wall. The lettering was outlined beautifully in pencil but only a small portion of it had been painted. Nick squinted and read it aloud. "Welcome to the ProcrastiNation."

Max shook his head. "The paint is sitting right there, too. Sad place. So much potential, so few results. Inaction in action everywhere you look." Max moved forward, pointing to the piles. "See the roses over there? Those are 'I love you's' that people never said. The postcards? Vacations they always meant to take."

"The dumbbells and stationary bikes?"

"Exercises they kept promising to do."

They stopped near Gunther and watched him restack his pile. His bulging muscles threatened to tear through his T-shirt with every flex. Nick greeted him as he paused to catch his breath.

"Quite a physique. You must have used every piece of equipment in your pile."

"Don't have time to use 'em," Gunther grunted. "Too busy stackin 'em." He lifted an entire treadmill over his head and tossed it atop the heap. "Gonna get myself a more meaningful job ... one of these days."

Nick stepped back and surveyed his surroundings. He felt sadness for all the things that would never be done and a growing desire to remedy the situation.

Max's desire lay elsewhere. "My stomach's starting to growl. Let's go."

Nick protested. "We can't. Not now."

"We can't? Not now?" Max laughed. "You've

been here too long, Nick. You're starting to sound like a citizen."

"I'm not going to act like one, though."

"What are you going to do?"

"I'm going to take some action. Somebody's got to tell these people that 'Someday' is not a day of the week!"

Realizing he was still holding the clipboard, Nick waved it in the air and called for the foreman. Nick spoke to him for several moments before the foreman interrupted and snatched the clipboard back.

"Look pal, I'm not authorized to change the delivery date. I'll put this 'Someday' concept on the back burner. The stuff has to stay here for the time being."

"For the what?" Max asked.

"For the time being," the man snapped.

"Good heavens! That's me!"

Max pulled open his coat and pointed to a golden badge pinned to the inside. His name was printed in royal purple, his title in brilliant red. "Maximillion: The Time Being."

Nick spoke, a grin slowly forming on his face. "So ... they've been keeping all this stuff here ... for you?"

"Looks that way." Max gave Nick a wink and turned to the foreman. "I'd like to make a little change in the delivery date, if you don't mind."

He passed his hand over the clipboard and the word "Someday" faded away. The word "Today" reappeared in its place. The foreman's eyes went wide.

"To-today?" he stammered. "I-I'm not sure my men can get everything done today."

"Sure they can," Max said. "They just need a little direction."

"What kind of direction?"

"How about ... forward!"

Max snapped his fingers and the motion of the entire room shifted. Trucks that were backing into the warehouse switched gears and pulled away. Workers who were unloading crates began reloading them. Objects that had been piled high were being dragged down, dispersed, and prepared for delivery.

The foreman flashed a nervous smile, flipped through his papers, and frantically began crossing items off his list. He hurried off and vanished in the flurry of activity.

Nick and Max watched the workers for several minutes. When the warehouse was nearly empty, they turned and headed for the exit.

"That was impressive," Nick said. "Why did you decide to help?"

"It seemed important to you," Max explained. "If something is important, take action. All we truly have is now. Someday may never come."

Nick nodded. "So what do we do with our now ... now?"

"We go and get a milkshake!"

Max opened the door and led Nick out of the warehouse. They crossed the street and headed for a 1950s-style diner.

"The Island Diner," Max said as they entered. "Best shakes in the world."

Customers lined the counter laughing and enjoying lunch. Waitresses worked the booths, shouting out numbers to the short-order cook. Doo-wop music drifted from a jukebox where high school sweethearts held hands and searched for their favorite song. Max sat down in a booth, leaned back, and pressed his head into the cushion. Nick sat across from him, leaned forward, and pressed him for answers.

"Why do you need a milkshake now?"

"I feel like treating myself."

"Can we get it to go, at least?"

"To go? Where do we need to go?"

"To the next chime. I got this one."

"Oh, you have?"

"Well, the bell hasn't rung yet, but it's pretty clear. Don't procrastinate. Carpe diem."

"Gather ye rosebuds while ye may."

Nick turned at the sound of a woman's voice. A gray-haired waitress stood beside the table, the beauty of her youth still radiating behind her tired eyes and wrinkled skin. She repeated the line and completed the verse.

"Gather ye rosebuds while ye may, Old Time is still a-flying; and this same flower that smiles today, Tomorrow will be dying."

There was a hint of sadness as she spoke, but she smiled as she finished. "Robert Herrick. Learned that poem a long time ago," she said as she handed Nick a menu. "I thought it might help you make your point."

Max cleared his throat to get her attention. "It was a lovely poem, Rosemary."

She turned and smiled softly. "An old poem for an old friend." She slid him a menu. "It's always a pleasant surprise when you stop by."

"You know I can't stay away too long. Something about this place always brings me back."

"The food?" she asked playfully.

"The food … and the pretty girl who serves it."

Max gave Rosemary a wink. Rosemary hid her blushing face. Nick shook his head and smiled.

"Maybe she should sit here," he said, pretending to offer his seat. "You can get one of those shakes … with two straws."

Rosemary laughed and took back Max's menu.

"So you came in for a shake? Should have known." She turned to Nick. "A sweet talker with a sweet tooth, that's what he is. Shall I bring you a shake, too? Chocolate is the house specialty."

Nick handed her his menu. "That sounds great. Thanks."

"I'll be right back then."

Max watched her as she walked away. Nick watched Max and laughed.

"I don't believe it."

"Don't believe what?"

"You were flirting with her."

"I was paying her some attention."

"By flirting."

"I don't see Rosemary as often as I wish. When I am with her, I want her to know how special she is. I simply gave her my full attention."

"Well, there was definitely some chemistry there. I think you should ask her out."

"If you must know, I plan on doing just that."

"When? Someday?"

"No. Today."

Max swept a hand through his hair in an attempt to tame it. He tugged the bottom of his vest, sat up straight, and stared at the door. Rosemary came out of the kitchen.

"Here she comes," Nick whispered. "Seize the date."

"There you go, gentlemen," she said as she set down the shakes. "Consider yourselves lucky."

"With you as our waitress, how could we not?"

Nick shook his head at the old man's smooth comment. Rosemary did the same.

"We were nearly out of ice cream," she explained. "I had just enough left to make two shakes. If you hadn't come in when you did, you would have missed out."

Nick eyed Max. "It would be a shame to miss out on something so sweet, wouldn't it?" He leaned his head to point to Rosemary, concealing the gesture by taking a sip.

Max looked at Nick and took his cue.

"Rosemary, I was thinking of coming back into town soon, to do a little fishing."

She turned and gave Nick a wink. "Sounds like he's using a line already."

Nick continued sipping his shake, pretending not to be paying attention.

Max regained Rosemary's attention. "I was wondering

if I could call you when I'm here. I was hoping to take you out on the town."

"Well, it's about time you asked," she said. "I was beginning to think I'd lost my charm. I'd be honored."

Rosemary excused herself and walked away. Max looked to Nick and spoke.

"What do you think?"

"I think she's sweet."

"I know she's sweet. That's why I asked her out. What do you think of the shake?"

Nick sipped deeply and smiled as he came up for air. "Ahhh! Best I ever had."

"Told you so. Take your time and enjoy it."

Nick looked down at his glass. "Errr, too late."

"What do you mean?"

Nick swirled his straw around the cup, then looked up. "I was trying to keep myself busy during your little love connection there. Looks like I only have about a sip left."

"Well, you can enjoy that."

"No, I can't."

"Why not?"

Nick let the straw fall into the cup. He sat back and sighed. "It's too depressing."

"What's too depressing?"

"Final sips. I hate them. The drink slides up the straw. The air slides in. And that slurp sneaks out like a little laugh letting you know it's over. It's the saddest sound in the whole world."

"You've thought about this before."

"I hate the feeling of knowing that something good is over. When I finish this sip, the shake will be gone. I drank it too quickly, and I can't order another one. I can look back at my life and see the same pattern: Great moments that went by too fast, opportunities I won't get again."

"Look at you. You're upset over things that are gone. You're worrying about things that might not come. You've got to just relax, and be."

"Be what?"

"Be. Just exist. Practice patience. Focus on the moment at hand and nothing else."

"That's difficult."

"Sure it is, but you can teach yourself to do it."

He leaned forward and finished the last sip of his shake. Nick flinched a bit at the sound, but Max just smiled a smile of satisfaction. "I want you to take the last sip of your shake now. I want you to enjoy it for what it is."

"But … "

"No buts. I don't want you to be one second in the past or one second in the future. I just want you to be here. The greatest moments in life are the ones we spend 'in the moment.' Moments we enjoy without concern. Rejoicing in a moment of victory. Singing along with our favorite song. Laughing with someone we really love. Those are the moments we are truly alive."

"You're telling me to live without thinking?"

"I'm telling you to live. There are times to prepare for the future. There are times to reflect on the past. But there are times to simply enjoy the present."

"Here's a present for you to enjoy," Rosemary said, returning to the table with the check. "The milkshakes are on the house."

She turned to Max, and Nick watched them share a silent moment. The look in his eyes, the warmth in her smile, and the tender touch of their fingers as she handed him the bill spoke volumes.

Nick closed his eyes and took a sip. He felt the rich chocolate flavor running over his taste buds. He felt the coldness tickling his tongue. His toe tapped in tune with the song on the jukebox, and the happiness he felt for Max filled his own heart with hope. He enjoyed the moment for what it was.

Nick's eyes opened at the sound of a bell.

Rosemary looked over her shoulder. "Sounds like an order's up. I'd better run." She winked at Max. "And I'd better hear from you soon."

Rosemary waved goodbye and hurried away. Nick looked at the table and saw her name and phone number written on the back of the check.

"So, you got a date."

Smitten, Max smiled and changed the subject. "And you got a chime."

He turned the check over and slid it to Nick. "Chime Six is in the middle of the clock. In the middle of your day and in the middle of any activity, be in the moment. Practice patience. All you truly have is now."

Nick pulled his watch from his pocket and read the back of the check.

⋆⟞ CHIME 6 ⟻⋆

TIME IN THE MOMENT

*I appreciate the simple pleasures
of daily living.*

I take action on the most important things first.

*When I am with people,
I give them my full attention.*

I practice patience.

Nick saw the number six appear on the face of his watch. He held it up for Max to see, but realized he had already left the table.

He walked outside to find his friend admiring the setting sun as it spread fiery light across the seashore.

"Isn't it wonderful?" Max whispered. He beckoned Nick to join him on a bench facing the horizon. The old man smiled playfully. "I collect sunsets."

"How?"

"I save them in my memory. Watching the sun go down is my favorite time to be in the moment."

Nick opened his mouth to speak. Max raised a hand. "Shhh. Just watch."

Gorgeous beams of light played upon the waves as the sun inched closer to the horizon. The final rays skipped across the water until they sparkled in the old man's eyes. Max stood with renewed energy.

"Congratulations, Nick. You're half way home!"

Nick smiled. "Time flies when you're having fun."

"Speaking of flying," Max said. "Our ride's right out back!"

SKY'S NOT the LIMIT

NICK FOLLOWED MAX AROUND THE BACK OF THE diner and was surprised to see a small runway stretching out in the distance. A two-seat, single-engine plane started up noisily, its engine sputtering, its propeller spinning.

Nick grew nervous as they drew nearer. "Do we have to fly to Chime Seven?"

"Seven is a magical number, Nick. We can explore the seven continents. We can sail the seven seas. We can visit the Seven Wonders of the World."

They reached the plane, which looked even more rickety than Nick had imagined. Though the peeling paint and patched-up frame caused Nick concern, Max approached it with confidence. He gathered some equipment from the top of a wing and handed Nick an old-fashioned, leather flight cap and a pair of goggles. "Put these on and hop in!"

Max climbed into the pilot's seat. Nick settled into the seat behind him, shouting as he buckled the weathered straps under his chin. "Are you sure this thing is safe?"

"I don't know," Max called back. "I've never flown it before!"

Max picked up a small book then placed it in his lap out of Nick's view. Nick hoped he wasn't reading flight instructions for the first time.

After several minutes, the plane suddenly and unexpectedly took off. It rocketed skyward at a surprisingly rapid pace before straightening out and settling into a steady pattern. Nick was thrilled by the experience of sitting in the open cockpit.

He relaxed and enjoyed the view.

He reveled at the sound of the roaring engine.

He smiled at the coolness of fresh air rushing by his face.

He panicked at the sight of a mountain standing directly in their path.

"Look out!" Nick shouted, pounding Max on the shoulder and pointing forward. "We're going to crash!"

"No. We're going to land."

"You can't land on a mountain! It's impossible!"

"Anything is possible!"

Max pulled the plane into an upward climb, looped upside down and soared straight for the mountaintop. Nick shut his eyes and awaited for the inevitable crash.

What he got was a small thud.

He opened his eyes to see that Max had landed the plane on the peak of the mountain. It balanced upon the pointy tip, swaying slightly in the breeze.

Nick marveled at the plane's positioning. "How did you know you could do that?"

"I didn't know." Max looked back and lifted his goggles. "But you can't achieve the impossible if you don't attempt it."

Max hopped out of his seat and stood on a wing. Nick's heart raced. He was certain Max's weight would tilt the plane and tumble it down the mountainside.

"What are you doing?" Nick shouted. "Get back in your seat!"

"I can't."

"Why not!"

"Because *you're* in my seat." Max paced from one wing to the other. "I can't sit down until you move."

"Where am I supposed to go?"

Max pointed to the pilot's seat. "Up here." The plane took a sudden tilt towards the left wing on which he stood. Max turned casually, narrowly averting disaster, and walked the other way. "You'd better hurry."

Nick jumped from his seat and crawled into the one vacated by Max. Max climbed into the one abandoned by Nick. The plane settled down, balancing perfectly yet precariously atop the peak.

Max buckled himself in. "Okay. Let's go!"

"Go?" Nick shouted, looking at the controls. "I don't

know how to fly a plane!"

"You don't want to be stuck in the same place forever, do you?"

"Of course not."

"Find a way to get yourself going then." He reached out his arms and patted the plane. "Do you know what makes this plane move, Nick?"

"I'm guessing fuel."

"Then you're guessing wrong. This is a plane that is powered by dreams. Focus on your dreams, and you'll soar to new heights."

Nick paused to consider Max's words. Max posed a question.

"Why do you think some people achieve their dreams while others don't?"

"Well, I think that luck plays a role."

"If you think that dreams are achieved by luck, I have seven words for you. 'Good luck is where preparation meets opportunity.'"

Nick repeated the words, raising a finger as he said each one.

Max pointed around and spoke. "Too many people

go through life with their head in the clouds. They get stuck in place waiting for their dreams to come out of the blue. All they need is a little preparation to get themselves going."

"So, what do I do?"

"First, you must see the invisible. See your dreams in your mind's eye. Imagine your dreams with as much detail as you can. Then, this next part is critical." Nick was taking in every word. Max paused, then spoke. "Make the invisible visible. Writing your ambitions on paper is the first step in turning your dreams into reality. When I see my dreams in writing, they become more real. It's the first step in the journey. All you do then is make your dreams more visible each day through action, and before you know it, you are living your dreams. Do you see my book up there?"

Nick nodded and picked it up, surprised to see the pages empty.

"It's a flight log," Max explained. "Take a moment and think about your plans, your dreams. Put them on paper, and you'll start moving."

"What kind of dreams?"

"All kinds. Goals you'd like to accomplish. Places you'd like to explore. Adventures you'd like to take. Think about yourself, your family. Shoot for the stars."

Max waved his hand and the afternoon sky began to change. The blue faded to black, and the brightness of the sun gave way to the brilliance of the stars. Max pointed to a pattern of seven stars. They flashed brighter, distinguishing themselves from the rest.

"Do you know the name of that constellation?"

Nick shook his head, marveling at the majesty of the evening sky. "I know the Big Dipper and the Little Dipper. It's not one of those."

"It's Pleiades: The Seven Sisters. A favorite of poets." Max recited Tennyson from memory. "'Many a night I saw the Pleiades, rising thro' the mellow shade, Glitter like a swarm of fire-flies tangled in a silver braid.'"

"It's beautiful. I guess I never heard of it."

"That's okay. We have a lovely constellation prize for you!"

Max gestured toward the evening sky and a

shadow appeared in the distant starlight. A faint sound of flapping wings grew in intensity as Nick leaned forward, straining to see what it was. Moments later, something burst from the darkness, flying into Max's outstretched arms.

Nick assumed it was some type of small bird until Max extended his hands to reveal a small, gold box. The top was adorned with elegant gems fashioned in the shape of a seven. Two white wings, like those of a cherub, extended from the sides of the box, dancing as they draped over Max's wrist. The box levered itself open and revealed its contents: a golden pencil resting on a purple satin pillow.

"Use this," Max said, "to write down your dreams."

Nick watched, thrilled and bewildered.

"It is a number seven pencil," Max explained. "The pencil of dreams. It contains the seven colors of the rainbow, the seven musical notes of the scale, and the power of all seven days of the week. The moment you place the tip on the paper, it will reveal your greatest desires. It knows no bounds. It believes in all the possibilities of you."

Nick stared at the pencil, unsure whether he was ready to handle such an extraordinary instrument.

"Go on," Max encouraged. "Take it. Put your dreams on paper. Make the invisible visible. Set your dreams in motion."

Nick reached his hand forward and took the pencil into his fingertips. Gripping it, he took a deep breath in anticipation of the first words. He lowered his hand slowly and began to write. "I will … "

The next few moments were a blur. Thoughts flowed from his mind faster than Nick ever imagined they could. Plans for getting promoted, dreams for his daughter's education, and fantasies about family vacations poured onto the page. Nick stopped and looked truly alarmed. "Now what do I do? I ran out of lead!"

Max opened the winged box and produced a sparkling, ruby pencil sharpener. "I think we can manage."

Nick excitedly sharpened the pencil and wrote even more zealously than before. Pausing for a moment between pages, Nick noticed the plane was no longer resting on the mountain. With each dream he had committed to paper, it had risen like a hot air balloon so that it hovered in the air, high above the mountaintop.

"Your dreams are beginning to take flight," Max explained. "Keep writing. Let them soar."

Faster and faster, page after page, Nick listed goals from every area of his life. The pencil defined his dreams as if it had a mind of its own, making Nick wish he had happened upon the magic pencil years before. He was writing and sharpening at a feverish pace when he stopped and held the book up for Max to see.

"Am I writing too much?" he asked hesitantly. "I mean, these are real ambitions, dreams I've always wanted to live. But it's not going to be possible for me to do them all."

"You can't have everything," Max explained. "But you can have anything. Taking time to dream allows you to focus on the 'anything' that you want."

Nick returned to the book, suddenly realizing that he was running out of lead again. The writing and re-sharpening had reduced the number seven pencil to a tiny stub.

"I … I think I killed your magic pencil." Nick held it up and watched Max take it. "You can fix it though, right? You can do your magic and make it new again."

"I'm afraid I can't." Max placed the pencil stub and sharpener back into the gold box.

"You have another number seven pencil then?"

"That is … was … the only one." Max released the box as one would release a pigeon. The two men watched it soar into the night sky.

"What do I do now? I still have dreams to list."

Max patted his pockets and pulled out a worn, yellow pencil. He handed it to Nick. "Excuse the teeth marks. I tend to chew on them sometimes."

"I can't use this. This is just an ordinary pencil."

Max smiled and stared at Nick. Nick started to complain again, then stopped. "The other pencil was ordinary, too, wasn't it?"

Max nodded. "You're the one who is extraordinary, Nick. Look at the dreams you've listed, the possibilities you've imagined. A pencil only has power when you take the time to use it, and believe."

Nick put the yellow pencil to the paper and continued listing his dreams. He glanced around as he wrote, watching the plane rise toward the stars. He added more dreams to the list: dreams that had remained dormant, plans that had been pushed aside by other priorities. When Nick finished, he handed the book and pencil to Max.

"Done! For now, anyway. I can always dream bigger. The sky's the limit, right?"

Max smiled. "The sky's only the beginning! There's more beyond the sky!"

"Well, it looks like we reached it. What do we do now?"

"We move forward."

Nick glanced at the cockpit. "There's only one control up here. I just push it forward and we'll go, right?"

"We will if you're ready."

"I'm ready!" Nick lowered his goggles, thrust the control forward, and braced himself for the burst of speed.

The engine roared. Nick cheered. The plane stayed still.

"We're not moving," he called back.

"Take some action."

"What do I need to do? Step on the gas? Release a brake?"

"Write some steps."

"Write what?"

"Write some steps." Max flipped through the book. "You want your dreams to move forward, but you've got no direction, no plan." He handed the book and pencil back to Nick. "You've got your dreams off the ground. That's a great start. But in order to go forward, you've got to give them some effort."

Nick took the book and opened it. "What do I do?"

"Read me one of your dreams."

Nick looked at the page in front of him. "I'd love to build my own house."

"That's a wonderful dream. It's bold. It's ambitious. What's the first step?"

"I could research designs and study houses I like."

"Perfect. Write it down!"

Nick jotted the words on the page and the plane eased forward.

"We're in motion," Max cheered. "What else can

you do?"

"I can … ask Alicia to help me sketch out some ideas. I could talk to some local firms … Oh! One of my clients is an architect."

"Perfect!"

Nick wrote quickly and the plane picked up speed. Max placed his hands behind his head and leaned back in his seat.

"You're pulling your dreams from your heart. You're focusing them in your mind. And you're taking action with your body. Keep working. I'm going to enjoy the ride."

Nick continued writing. Some of the steps were obvious; others were creative, even risky. Each one made the path a little clearer, propelling the plane a little farther.

They had traveled a great distance when Nick paused and addressed his passenger.

"We're cruising pretty steady here. But we don't seem to be getting any closer to landing anywhere."

"Ah, I was wondering when you'd notice."

"I've got to add something else to my book, don't I?"

"If you want to land this plane, you need a destination. A pilot never flies without knowing where he is going to land. Read me another dream."

Nick read from the page he was working on. "Take the family to Europe."

"Sounds nice. You have steps planned out?"

Nick consulted his list. "Start a special savings account. Get suggestions from friends who've traveled abroad."

"Great! When do you plan to go?"

"Someda ... I mean, I don't know. Summer. When Grace's out of school."

"Which summer?"

"Summer after next, I guess. We could go for our twentieth wedding anniversary."

"Now, there's a plan! Put the deadline next to the dream."

Nick did as Max said and the plane drifted downward. He smiled and began writing dates next to the others as well.

Max leaned forward and offered advice. "We need timetables to let us know whether or not we're on target. Be realistic when you write them, but be optimistic, too. Set dates that are feasible but also encourage you to take action."

Nick placed deadlines by each of his dreams, set the book aside, and prepared for landing. A city skyline appeared on the horizon.

"Does that city have a place for me to land?"

"I certainly hope so, because that's where we're headed. Chime Seven reminds you to dream and believe that anything is possible. Think about, take action toward, and live your dreams each of the seven days of the week."

Max handed him a postcard of the exact skyline. The words "Infinity City" were written in italics across the front. Nick looked up, scanning the maze of skyscrapers for a barren spot to use as a landing strip. Veering left, he soared over smaller homes and headed for an open field. The plane buzzed over a herd of grazing cows, startling them and sending them running. Their cowbells clamored as they scattered for cover. Nick's eyes fell upon the back of the postcard.

⇒ CHIME 7 ⇐

TIME TO DREAM

I believe my potential can be greater.

*I clearly define my goals in writing
and put deadlines on them.*

I take action toward my goals daily.

Many of my dreams have come true.

Nick grabbed his watch and saw the number seven appear. He looked forward and screamed. The plane dived. He clamped his eyes shut and awaited the impact.

The Funny Glasses

DEATH WAS A STRANGE SENSATION. NICK FELT HIMSELF lunging forward and then backward as if riding on a pendulum. His mind was trying to fathom what had happened when Max's voice let him know they had both survived.

"Open your eyes. We've arrived!"

Nick peeled his eyelids open and discovered the reason behind the rocking. Although he was still on a plane, it had somehow changed form. Smaller, and no longer capable of flight, it was attached to the top of a large, metal spring that wobbled up from the ground.

A child's voice shouted out from behind him, "You look silly, mister!"

Nick turned his body toward the voice, sending the plane rocking wildly. He fought to regain his balance, tumbled out onto soft grass, and looked up. A little girl no older than five hopped down from a spring rocking horse. She roared with laughter and ran off. Max stepped into view, offered a hand, and helped Nick to his feet.

"Nice landing," he said. "On both accounts."

Nick brushed himself off. His bottom was bruised as well as his ego. He looked around to see where he was.

It was a playground in a shady park on the outskirts of the city. Children ran between the slides and swings. Adults peppered nearby benches. A trio of older gentlemen sat gathered around a small table. Two of them focused on a game of chess; the third puffed a cigar, waiting to challenge the victor.

"There he is! There he is!"

The little girl from the rocking horse returned,

accompanied by two boys of slightly larger sizes. Max squatted down and brushed the blonde hair from the little girl's eyes. "Good to see you again, Sophie." He stood and turned to the boys, greeting them both with a secret handshake. "Sammy. Steven. This is my friend Nick."

Sophie tugged Steven's shirt and pointed with her tiny fingers. "That's the funny man who fell off the plane."

Nick looked uncomfortably at the children. He didn't like the way they stared up at him, and he certainly wasn't amused at being referred to as "the funny man." The older boy stepped up and spoke. "Can you do it again, mister? Sammy and I were on the monkey bars, and we missed it."

"No!" Nick snapped a little more than he meant to. He softened his voice, but maintained his seriousness. "I don't have time to play right now."

"Aw, he's no fun." Sammy kicked the dirt and turned away. He sprinted across the park, calling as he ran. "Last one to the slide is a rotten egg!"

Steven turned and chased after him. Sophie

looked at Nick with sad eyes, walked away slowly, and sat alone on a seesaw.

Nick bowed his head. "I didn't mean to make her so sad. I'm just not in the mood to play around."

"There's always time to play, Nick."

"We're just a little busy right now."

"That's when we need Chime Eight the most. We need a little fun to take the edge off of our responsibilities." Max pointed to Sophie. "Sit with her. I want to show you something."

Nick moved toward the tiny girl. She sat on the seesaw, touching the ground, staring up at the empty seat on the opposite end.

"It's not going to work. I'm too heavy."

"Trust me." Max encouraged.

Nick shrugged and placed his hand on the raised side of the seesaw. Sophie's pout faded slowly as he spoke.

"Mind if I sit here?"

"You gonna play?"

"I'm gonna try."

Sophie smiled. Nick lowered his side of the seesaw,

raising her gently. He straddled the seat and stood so that he and Sophie were level.

Max tapped Nick's leg. "Lift your feet."

"You want me to crash to the ground?"

Sophie laughed in anticipation. "Do it! Do it!"

"You heard the young lady."

Nick winced at the loudness of her shouts. "Everybody heard her."

Sophie's voice caught the attention of her brothers. They hurried to her side to see the cause of the commotion. Steven arrived first.

"What's going on over here?"

Max greeted him with a grin. "Nick here is about to do a trick."

"He gonna make my sister disappear?" Sammy laughed at his own joke. Sophie stuck out her tongue and turned to Nick.

"I'm ready, mister! Lift your feet!"

Max nodded. The children clapped. Nick lifted his legs.

The moment seemed to move in slow motion. Nick grimaced, preparing himself for the fall. The children cheered, awaiting the same event with far more enthusiasm. Max watched calmly, knowing full well it would never come.

Nick sat, stunned, looking across at Sophie: her weight balancing his weight perfectly, the seesaw magically remained in position.

"Cool!"

"How are you doing that?"

The boys screamed in delight, dancing around the seesaw. Sophie smiled proudly, bowing from her seated position. Max leaned in, speaking softly amongst the racket.

"Having fun?"

"Yeah. It feels good."

"It's the perfect balance between work and play. Achieving it is always rewarding." He paused for a moment to watch the children. "Are you worried about the things you need to do?"

"Not at the moment."

"Then I've made my point." He reached up and plucked Sophie from her seat. Nick plummeted quickly, planting his feet to prevent his bottom from crashing to the ground. The children giggled, gathering around Max.

"We all need a diversion, Nick. Whether it's sailing or skiing, baseball or board games."

"Chime Eight. Time to play." Nick stepped off the seesaw. "Am I right?"

"You're right."

Nick placed a hand on Max's shoulders and smiled. "Then … you're it!"

He shuffled off, shooing the children as he did. They cackled and scattered in every direction. Max let loose a hearty laugh and headed after them.

The game of tag lasted longer than Nick expected. He lost himself in the pure joy of play until he began to feel winded. When a number of new children joined in, he and Max begged out and settled on a bench. They watched the children play as they caught their breath.

"Good game," Max said.

"Great game," Nick replied. "Wore me out, but it was worth it."

"You were enjoying life instead of just passing

through. Remember this when you get back home."

Nick sighed. "I'd like to. But it's not like I can play all day long."

"No, but you can have a playful spirit." Max waved toward the gentlemen at the chess table. "Harry," he shouted. "Help me out here a second."

A man with white whiskers excused himself and headed over. His companions bid him goodbye, barely looking up from their game. Max stood and greeted him as he arrived.

"How goes the chess games, Harry?"

"They are matches, not games. Those guys are just playing for a chance to lose to me later." Harry tipped his golf cap toward Nick. He chewed his cigar as a gruff voice sneaked out of the side of his mouth. "You play?"

Nick stood and smiled. "I'm working on it."

"I'm teaching Nick how to have more fun," Max said. "Helping him to see the humor all around him. You have something that can help us out?"

"I've got just the number!" Harry puffed his cigar and removed it from his mouth. He looked into the nothingness before him, pursed his lips into the shape of an 'O' and blew out two immaculate rings of smoke. They glided toward Nick, one taking position above the other, widening as they traveled together. Harry pointed proudly to his creation.

"A perfect figure eight. I give it a ten!" He gestured to Max, inviting the next move. "She's all yours."

Max nodded, reached up with one hand, and plucked the number eight out of the air. He turned it on its side and waved it back and forth like a fan.

Nick was marveling at the fact that it was maintaining its shape when he saw that it was slowly becoming solid. Before he could comment, the figure eight had magically refashioned itself into a pair of eyeglasses.

"How ... how did you do that?"

"He did it pretty well if you ask me!" Harry laughed, pointing to the glasses with his cigar. "It was quite a spectacle."

Max shook his head and held out the glasses. "These are number eight glasses, Nick. When you look through them, you can see humor in everything.

Even in lousy jokes like Harry's. Try them on."

Nick slid the glasses in place and looked around. Everything seemed blurry. "They're messing up my eyes."

"They're opening up your mind. Your eyes just need a moment to adjust."

Nick looked again and saw the objects around him shift into focus. "That's a little better. I'm not sure things look different, though."

"Let's give them a little test run then. I want you to look for humor in an everyday situation." Max perused the park. "Do you see the man walking his dog?"

Nick nodded. He could see the man walking slightly ahead of his pet. He noted what seemed to be a smile on the dog's face. "What do you want me to do?"

"Imagine what the dog is thinking."

"He's thinking that he is in control, that he has the man on a leash."

Harry snickered. Max patted Nick on the back. "Not bad. Let's try another one." He pointed toward a series of benches scattered on both sides of a sidewalk. "What do you see over there?"

A man in sunglasses sat on a bench reading a newspaper. A woman across from him tossed popcorn to a gathering group of pigeons.

"The man accidentally left his lunch at home. He's pretending to read the paper, but he's secretly plotting to steal the woman's popcorn."

"And the woman?"

"The popcorn's left over from a matinee. She just saw an old Alfred Hitchcock movie. If any more birds show up, she's going to be *in* an old Hitchcock movie."

Harry leaned toward Max. "The kid's good."

Nick slid the glasses down, peeking over the lenses at Max. "This is kind of fun. Why didn't I see this stuff before?"

"You just weren't looking. Humor surrounds you all the time, Nick. Choose to open your eyes. The glasses are helping you right now, but they're just training glasses. With a little practice, you won't need them at all."

Harry pointed to a man at the chess table. One of the men stood up, stomped his feet, and threw his cap to the ground. "Now, that's funny."

Nick watched and wondered aloud. "He's upset because he lost?"

"He's upset because he won," Harry said as he headed back. "He knows he has to play me now!"

"Take it easy on him, Harry," Max shouted. "Thanks for the help."

"My pleasure." Harry tipped his cap as he walked away. "Good luck, kid. Have fun."

"Will do." Nick turned to Max. "What now?"

"Well, it's easy to have fun in the park. Let's head into town and see what happens."

Max stopped when they reached the front gate of the park.

"When I open this gate," Max explained, "we are going to be on the main street of the city. We're going to run into random people."

"You want me to find something funny about them?"

"No. I want you to look for the kid inside them.

Your glasses will help you see them."

Max stepped through the gate and turned the corner. Nick did the same, anticipating a parade of children, tiny bodies draped in adult clothing, bustling about on their daily business.

All he saw were adults.

He adjusted the glasses. He stared harder. He turned to Max and sighed. "I don't see the kid in anyone."

"Look closer, Nick. Seek out the clues. The skip in a step. The enthusiasm in a voice. The twinkle in an eye." Max pointed down the sidewalk to a series of small shops. "Think of it as a game of hide-and-seek. Go see who you can find."

Nick walked slowly, watching people as they passed. Max tapped him on the shoulder and pointed to an old woman on the other side of the street.

"There," he said, "watch her."

The old woman carried a sunflower-shaped parasol to shield her from the sun. She held it high as she walked past the storefronts, but lowered it every few steps as she moved under the small, shaded awnings in front of the doors. The rise and fall of the giant flower was attracting all sorts of attention. The faint smile on the woman's face hinted she was doing it for just that reason.

She crossed to Nick's side of the street, and headed toward him, maintaining the perfect rhythm of her parasol ritual.

Max pointed to the door ahead of Nick. "She's headed for the beauty shop. Show her that you've seen her playful spirit."

"What do I do?"

"Meet her at the door. Do something unexpected. Catch her off guard."

The word "guard" gave Nick a sudden burst of inspiration. He sped forward, swung open the door, and bowed grandly like a palace doorman.

"This way, M' lady."

Nick's attempt at a British accent was laughable. When the woman paused, unsure what to make of his actions, he glanced up, still in full bow, and smiled.

The woman relaxed and returned the favor. "Thank you, kind sir." Her royal accent was equally poor. She closed her parasol and tapped it on the top of Nick's shoulders. "I knight thee and bid thee good day."

She slipped inside. Nick turned to address Max when he heard a crash. A young woman had stumbled as she stepped out of the grocer's. The contents of her bag spilled onto the sidewalk. Nick hurried to help her and greeted her over an upset carton of eggs.

"You gotta watch out for that gravity," he said, smiling. "It's everywhere."

She smiled back, embarrassed. "So are the eggs." Nick helped her collect the shattered shells and place them back into the carton. "Too bad I didn't buy a spatula. I could just whip up a meal right here."

Nick nodded. "A sidewalk soufflé. Sounds delicious. And I have just the dessert." He picked up a plastic container that had fallen on its top and presented it with flair. "Upside-down cake. Just open and serve. Should be a smashing success."

Nick placed the cake in the woman's bag and noticed a small milk carton had toppled into the street. He was about to step out and grab it when a delivery truck passed by, crushing it beneath its wheels.

"Let it go until traffic clears," the woman advised. "No use dying over spilled milk."

They laughed together for a moment, tossed the remaining items into her bag, and said goodbye. Max addressed him as he watched her walk away.

"Impressive, Nick. You found humor in the awkwardness of the moment. With a playful spirit, we can all laugh at the things that happen around us. Those funny things are life's way of taking the edge off our most challenging moments." He patted Nick's back as they started down the sidewalk. "This is a good chime for you. You've picked everything up very well."

"Everything but the eggs," Nick said pointing down. "Watch your step."

They strolled casually through the town. Nick took time to play with several strangers he met along the way. He was enjoying his walk immensely when he spied a tiny toyshop. He rushed to the window and marveled at the games, blocks, and puppets. Nick reached for the door, sighing when he found it locked.

"It's closed."

"But your mind is open. You don't need the toys to play."

Nick stepped back and stared. Moments from his youth rushed by like the toy train in the window. His eyes bounced from rubber balls to wind-up robots, each object bringing a memory more vivid than the last. He was smiling at a wooden sled, racing down a mountain in his mind, when his eyes fell upon the image of a little boy in the window.

Nick wondered for a moment how the boy had managed to get inside, then he realized it was merely a reflection. A cute young chap with a million dollar smile, he stood on the sidewalk beside Max. Nick noticed the boy's eyes wide with wonder and turned from the glass to greet him.

"So, which toy do you like best?"

Nick's voice trailed off. The boy was nowhere to be seen.

Max answered as if he were the one who had been addressed. "I'm a bit partial to the electric train. How about you?"

Nick looked back to the window. The reflection was still visible. He turned quickly to the sidewalk and saw nothing. He looked around and questioned Max with alarm.

"Did … did you just see a boy?"

Max answered calmly, still admiring the model railroad in front of him. "Where? When?"

"Here! A minute ago! Brown hair, about this tall."

Nick held his hand chest high. Max glanced over and nodded. "Oh, that boy. I saw him."

"Where?"

Max pointed to the window. "There."

Nick looked back slowly, seeing the reflection for the third time. It was a haunting illusion, but the image of the boy, so full of life, so innocent, gave Nick a strange sense of calm. He watched, wordless, afraid to turn away.

Max whispered so as not to startle him. "It's you."

Nick felt Max reach over and remove the glasses from his head. The image of the boy faded into the familiar shape of his forty-three-year-old reflection.

He sighed, exhaling his response.

"It is me."

Nick wanted another look. He turned to Max to ask for the glasses, but found his hands empty. Nick sighed as he spotted two smoke rings rising slowly into the air.

"You don't need them anymore, Nick. You can see him anytime you want."

Nick walked toward the window, watching his reflection approach from the other side. He spread his hands against the glass and, bringing his face close, he examined the wrinkles and receding hair, searching for signs of the child within.

A moment passed and the traces of a grin began tickling the corners of Nick's mouth. Pulling his hands from the window, he slid his thumbs into his ears and playfully pushed out his tongue. He laughed at the face in the glass. His younger self, striking the same goofy pose, laughed along.

Nick sighed and smiled. "Welcome back," he said. "I've missed you."

A bell sounded. Nick spun around to see the children

from the playground. Steven rode by, ringing the bell on his bike to get Nick's attention. Sammy walked behind him, pulling Sophie in a wagon.

Sophie hopped out and ran up to Nick. "Thanks for the fun, mister!"

Nick knelt down and smiled. "Thank you, Sophie."

"Want some gum, mister?"

Sophie opened her hand and revealed a piece of bubble gum. She spoke again, revealing wisdom beyond her years.

"Chime Eight reminds you not to take life too seriously. Make time to have fun and celebrate today. Time is your playground. Go play in it!"

She ran back to her brothers, waving as she rode off.

"Don't forget to read the comic!"

Nick opened the wrapper and slid the gum into his mouth. He looked down at the comic and smiled. It was the Eighth Chime. He took out his watch and read.

⇒ CHIME 8 ⇐

TIME TO PLAY

I see humor in everyday situations.

I laugh easily at myself.

I share my childlike enthusiasm with others.

I make time to have fun and
celebrate each day.

The number eight popped into place.

Max smiled. "Did you have fun?"

"Sure did. Where do we go next?"

"Uptown."

As if on cue, a rope ladder dropped from above, crashing to the sidewalk between them. Nick looked skyward and found that it had unfurled from a magnificent hot-air balloon.

Max took hold of the rope and began climbing.

"Come on," he shouted. "I'll give you a lift to work."

FINDING
IT

NICK CLIMBED ABOARD AND SETTLED IN AS THE BALLOON began its journey. It rose steadily, veering from the path of the street, drawing spirited waves and bewildered looks from townspeople passing below.

As small buildings began to give way to taller ones, Nick noticed that Max seemed to be controlling the wind more than the balloon itself. Max steered through the thickening city as if he were maneuvering through a maze, then thrust his hand forward.

"There it is!"

The wind shifted and the balloon soared for a distant building. A marvel of modern architecture, it was a massive structure of mirrored glass with two large letters towering from the rooftop. As the balloon touched down, Nick squinted skyward and read them.

"I.T.?"

"Institute of Technology." The men climbed from the balloon and Max secured it with a rope. "A conglomeration of the greatest scientific minds in the world. My old friend, Professor Flask, is in charge."

"Max calling the professor old?"

An elderly security guard greeted them from a doorway in the base of the towering metal "T." His shaggy white hair fell over his eyes like a mop placed on top of his head. "The boss should get a kick out of that."

Max laughed and rephrased his remark. "A *dear* friend of mine is in charge. Better?"

"Much better." The security guard cracked a smile as he led them inside. "It's good to see you, Max."

"Good to see you, too, Toby. Can you let Mel know I'm here?"

"Sure thing." He picked up a phone to place a call

but stopped in mid-motion. He replaced the receiver and pointed down the hallway. "Looks like she already knows."

Nick scrunched his face. "She?"

Max nodded and turned Nick by the shoulders. "She."

A slender woman in her early forties strolled toward them. Blonde bangs danced on her forehead just above the light blue rims of her rounded glasses. Her confident smile and graceful stride brought a hint of style to her simple white lab coat.

She slipped a tiny, spiral notepad into her coat pocket and gave Max a warm hug. "What a pleasant surprise. I saw you on the security camera."

"You look great, Mel. Always do."

"To what do I owe the pleasure of your visit?"

"I brought my friend Nick to meet you."

The woman turned to Nick and extended a hand. "Professor Flask," she said. "Melissa to my friends. Max is the only one who calls me Mel."

"I've been teaching Nick a few tricks," Max explained. "In fact, he's already come in contact with some of your greatest creations."

"I have?" Nick asked.

"The number eight glasses?" Max offered. "Mel's."

Nick raised an eyebrow. The professor nodded.

"That box that brought us the number seven pencil? Mel's."

Nick smiled. The professor nodded again.

"The recipe for that number six milkshake?"

Nick smiled. "Mel's?"

"No, that was Rosemary's. Mel's a great scientist, but she's a lousy chef."

The professor laughed at Max's joke. "He's right, you know. Wouldn't want to be a cook anyway."

"Why's that?" Nick asked.

"Following recipes? Filling out people's orders? Just doesn't do it for me."

"Rosemary seems to enjoy it."

"Well, that's the secret, isn't it? Working at something you enjoy." Flask headed down the hall, pointing through windows at various groups of scientists. "Now ... developing antidotes. Diagramming molecules. Dissecting bugs. These are things to get excited about."

"Sounds like you love your work."

"I don't consider what I do to be work. I consider it a way of life. If I won the lottery on Friday, I'd still be here on Monday."

There was a tap on the glass beside Flask as two scientists tried to catch her attention. The professor excused herself and moved through the door that led to the room.

Nick watched Flask greet the scientists. Though he couldn't hear the conversation, the excitement of the encounter was evident. There were smiles and handshakes followed by several awkwardly energetic high-fives.

Nick turned to Max. "She certainly is enthusiastic."

"That's part of her success. People love to work with her. It makes her unstoppable."

"It's too bad she can't harness that energy and market it."

"Harness the energy?" The professor had slipped out of the door and overheard the comment. "Remarkable idea!"

Nick smiled at the compliment.

The professor continued. "I had the same idea myself just the other day. Have nine of my best people working on it as we speak. Come on! I'll show you."

Flask headed down the hall and turned a corner. Max gave Nick a consoling look. "I told you she was unstoppable."

They hurried after the professor, finding her standing outside a room. Unlike the others, it had no window through which to view the activity within. The door, larger than those they had passed, seemed to be made of solid steel.

Nick was puzzled. "What's with the secrecy?"

"It's not secrecy that concerns me," Flask explained. "It's safety." She rapped on the door until a buzzer sounded to announce that they could enter. "Keep close to the wall. We don't want to contaminate anything."

The trio entered. Nine scientists in three rows of three looked up from their microscopes. They acknowledged the visitors momentarily then resumed work. They viewed slides and recorded results as the professor proudly narrated.

"The scientists in this room are working on a complex and potentially explosive endeavor. They are attempting to isolate and identify IT."

Nick's eyes narrowed with curiosity. "What's IT?"

"No one's exactly sure. That's what makes the process so fascinating." She looked to Max. "You want to help explain this?"

"IT is one of the secrets to success," Max offered. "A common component shared by those who find pure joy in their work."

Nick nodded. "The enthusiasm I said she should try to harness."

"Exactly!" Flask handed goggles to her guests. "Put these on. There could be a blast of energy at any moment."

Nick and Max did as instructed. Flask moved out among the scientists, gesturing for them to follow. Nick moved cautiously, watching the men and women remove drops of liquid from the beakers on their desks.

"What are they doing exactly?"

"They're studying successful people from all

walks of life: athletes, writers, builders, musicians, salespeople, teachers ... " She gently placed her hands on a man's shoulders. "Harold here is even studying me!"

He glanced up from his microscope and grinned. "If anyone's got IT, she does."

Flask blushed and moved along. "Once we isolate IT, we'll analyze IT."

"Then?"

"Then we share IT so everyone can feel the excitement of loving what they do."

Max interrupted, "Any breakthroughs so far?"

"We're close. I can feel it. We've narrowed our search to two critical areas: passion and talent. We just haven't found the right combination."

Nick pointed to the beakers. "What do you have them looking at?"

"Tears and perspiration." The professor lifted two beakers from a desk, presenting them as she spoke. "The tears represent passion. The desire a person has to succeed."

"The perspiration?"

"Talent: the effort put forth through special abilities." She set the beakers down and moved to a workstation.

"Where do you think IT lies, Nick?"

"I wouldn't know. I'm not a scientist."

"What are you?"

"I'm a salesman."

"Do you love what you do?"

"Well, I can't say I'm as enthusiastic as you are."

Max laughed. "No one's as enthusiastic as she is."

Flask rolled her eyes playfully, then focused back at Nick. "Answer truthfully. Do you love what you do?"

Nick contemplated the question, then nodded. "I'd have to say yes. I mean, I have an occasional down day, but most of the time, I'm pretty happy."

"Would you say you have IT?"

"I'd say there's a good chance."

The professor rubbed her hands together. "Let's experiment then. See if we can figure out the formula." She took an empty test tube from under the table and handed it to Nick. "This is for you. Let's find out what you're made of."

"I'll do my best," Nick said, "but I haven't done a science experiment since high school."

"I haven't stopped doing them since high school,

so it'll all even out."

Flask removed the spiral notepad from her pocket. "I'm going to ask some questions. I want you to respond quickly, with the first answers that pop into your head. Ready?"

"Ready."

"Why are you a salesman?"

"I just enjoy it. The travel. The clients. The money. It's like a daily adventure. I even get paid for it! Can't think of anything else I'd rather do."

"Sounds like passion!" Flask set her notebook aside and picked up a tiny eyedropper. She raised it to the edge of Nick's eye, brought it down to the test tube, and squeezed out a drop of liquid. "Just as I thought," she said proudly. "A single tear!"

Nick lifted the tube to get a closer look. Flask jotted some notes and spoke.

"Question two. What makes you successful?"

"I've just got a knack for it, I guess. Making the pitch. Closing the deal. Helping my clients. It all comes pretty easy."

"So you've got talent, too!"

Flask lifted the hair off Nick's forehead. "Aha!" She raised the dropper and collected a sample. She held it over the test tube and announced her findings as she added it to the mix. "A solitary bead of sweat!"

The contents of the test tube began to bubble. The professor grabbed her notepad. "It happens every time," she said, pointing to the test tube. "The passion and talent create momentum, but something's still missing." She sat down on the edge of the table. "I just wish I knew what it was."

Nick sat beside her and offered a thought. "Lots of people at my office have passion and talent. They don't seem as content as I do, though."

"What makes you more successful? What's the missing ingredient?"

"I wish I knew," Nick said. "I suppose I was just born to do it. Must be something in my blood."

"Eureka! That's it!" The professor leapt to her feet and grabbed her notes.

"What's it?"

"It's so obvious!" she said, scribbling joyously. "I don't know why we didn't see it before!"

"See what?" Nick turned to Max for answers. Max shrugged. Flask set down her pad and rolled a portable chalkboard to the front of the room and addressed the scientists.

"Ladies and gentlemen, I have an exciting announcement to make. Our visitor, Nick, has helped us stumble upon the formula for which we have all been searching."

Nick moved to the professor's side. "I have?"

The professor placed her arm around Nick and squeezed his shoulder. "No need for modesty, champ. No need at all." Flask tore open a sealed plastic wrapper and removed a button with the word "genius" printed on the front. She handed it to Nick then turned to the crowd. "Pay attention everyone. We're about to witness history!"

The scientists mumbled excitedly. Nick looked at the button and then handed it back to the professor. "I'm happy to have helped you out, but I don't think I deserve to wear this."

Flask looked surprised. She lifted the pin on the back of the button so it stuck straight into the air. "I don't want you to wear it. I want you to use it to prick your finger."

"You want my blood?"

"It's not just your blood, Nick. It's your destiny!"

The professor wiped the pin with alcohol and placed it back into Nick's hand. She picked up a clean test tube and held it out. "One drop. That's all I need."

Nick raised an eyebrow. Realizing the entire room was waiting on his action, he quickly obliged. The professor took back the test tube and turned to the crowd.

"There are many successful people in the world, but only a select few who experience pure joy in their work. They have the passion to succeed and the talent to do well, but they have the added bonus of finding a career they know they were born to do. These people have IT."

She poured the contents of the test tube into the first one and waited. The scarlet drop slid slowly along the glass. It danced on the lip of the container, as if it were taunting the onlookers, then dropped into the test tube below.

There was an instant burst of energy, a white-hot fire that erupted from the tube like a volcano. The scientists responded with equal explosiveness, cheering and applauding with fervor. Flask picked up some chalk and drew a diagram on the board. A "P" and a "T" side by side with a "D" balanced on top.

"IT," she explained, "is when Passion and Talent collide with Destiny!"

A work bell punctuated the air, sending the scientist scurrying in several directions..

Flask raised her voice above the clamor. "Ladies and gentlemen, our work here is done! It has been a day of great discovery! Dinner is on me!"

The scientists cheered again and began to exit, each of them taking a moment to thank Nick for his contributions. When they had cleared the room, Flask tapped Nick on the shoulder. "I want to thank you, too. For being part of the team."

"I didn't think a salesman would be much help in a science lab."

"It doesn't matter whether you're a salesperson, a waitress, or a scientist. If you do what you do with a passion to serve, with all the talents you bear, and with the commitment of following your destiny, you have IT." She looked at her notepad and smiled. "Blood, sweat, and tears. Who would have guessed?"

Flask tore a sheet from her notepad. "Chime Nine reminds you to do your work with purpose. Strive to build your talent. Work with passion." She presented the page to Nick. The Ninth Chime was scrawled across it. "Excuse the handwriting," she said. "I'm a bit better with equations."

Nick took out his watch and read.

⊷ CHIME 9 ⊶
TIME TO WORK

I strive to build my talents.
I have discipline to finish what I start.
I make good decisions with the money I earn.
I have passion for the work I do.

The number nine appeared in its place. Nick slipped the watch back into his pocket. Flask took Nick's hand in both of hers.

"Thank you again for all your help, Nick. If you ever want to try something new, we at I.T. would gladly welcome you aboard."

"Aboard?" Max's face went white. "Let's hurry, Nick. We're about to miss the train!"

TRAIN RIDE

NICK AND MAX BID THE PROFESSOR GOODBYE AND hurried from the building. The next thing Nick knew, they were running through a railway station. An old, black steam engine hissed smoke in the distance like a metal dragon.

"It's the number ten train," Max exclaimed, pointing to a painted number on the front of the engine. Max reached into his pocket and removed a single ticket .

"Here you go, Nick. I'll catch up with you later."

"You … you want me to go without you?"

"There's only one ticket."

"Let's buy another."

"You'll be fine. Trust me."

A shout of "All Aboard!" echoed through the station.

"I'm not going unless you do."

Max thrust the ticket into Nick's hand. "You can't miss this train, Nick."

"But … "

"Go!"

Nick turned and ran, sensing the urgency in Max's voice. Looking ahead, he spied a young man in a railroad uniform beckoning him from outside a passenger car. The conductor led him toward a door and Nick bounded into the train.

Two rows of red velvet seats stretched out before him, beautifully decorated and completely barren. Nick took a couple of steps and collapsed in a seat to contemplate the absence of passengers. Slowly realizing that he had not passed a single person while running for the train, he looked out the window. The entire station was eerily empty.

Nick turned as the conductor who had waved him onto the train stepped aboard. A dark-haired man in his mid-twenties, there was something about him that seemed oddly familiar. Nick wondered if his uniform, a suit and cap from an earlier era, reminded him of someone he had seen in an old movie.

"Ticket, please," the man asked, extending his hand.

"Where's this train going to take me?"

The conductor smiled as he took the ticket. "It will take you where you need to go." Tipping his cap, he turned and headed through the front of the car.

With a burst of sound and steam, the train pulled forward. Nick noticed Max waving from the platform. Still unsure why he was forced to catch the train on his own, Nick returned the wave, halfheartedly. When the train had cleared the station, he leaned back and watched the scenery change from city structures to country landscape. He was just about to close his eyes to rest when the train lurched and a terrible screeching emerged from the tracks below. The train came to a sudden stop, and the conductor rushed into the car.

"What's wrong?" Nick asked. "What's going on?"

"The train's carrying too much weight."

"But I'm the only passenger!"

"Oh no, it's not you. It's your baggage." The conductor moved past Nick and pushed open the door at the back of the car. "Why don't you come take a look?"

Nick rose from his seat and followed. They had walked through several empty passenger cars when the conductor stopped. "This is the first of the baggage cars. Be careful."

He opened the door and jumped back as a small suitcase tumbled toward him. Nick leaned in and peeked. He was astonished by what he saw. Suitcases of all sizes were stacked ceiling-high on both sides of the car. A thin path, barely wide enough to walk through, zigzagged down the middle.

Nick looked back at the conductor. "This doesn't make any sense. I'm the only one on the train."

"All the baggage is yours. You've been carrying it around for years."

Nick peeked in the door for a second time. "All this is mine?"

"And that isn't even half of it. I'd say it's time to let a few things go."

"What is all this stuff?"

"Things that have been weighing on your mind … slowing you down. Things to forgive others for."

"Like what?"

"Like this." He handed Nick the suitcase that had tumbled out of the pile. "You crammed it in right before you got on the train." The conductor pointed to a sticker on the side. "Track Ten," he read, "that's where you picked it up. You were angry that your friend only bought one ticket."

"I felt like he was abandoning me. I didn't see any reason for him not to come."

"We don't always see the reasons behind other people's actions. Do you think he was purposely trying to upset you?"

"No."

"Then lighten up. Forgive him so we can move on."

"Fine. I forgive him."

The conductor shook his head. "Really forgive him. You're just saying words."

Nick closed his eyes and thought. Everything Max had done so far had been with the best intentions. He sighed and said the words again, this time meaning them. "I forgive him."

Nick opened his eyes to see his hands empty. "Where's the suitcase?"

"It's gone," smiled the conductor. "Let's get rid of some more."

Nick moved hesitantly into the baggage car. "I'm supposed to forgive all these things?"

"Maybe not all, but most of them. Let's just start small and see what happens." He set a suitcase into Nick's hand and pointed to the sticker. "You've been carrying this one around since you were eleven years old. Something about a baseball card being destroyed by bicycle spokes?"

Nick laughed. "Lenny Freeman. I guess it's time I let that one go."

The two men continued through the car. Nick was surprised by the ill feelings he had built up over the years.

"Each one of them consumes energy," explained the conductor. "Free yourself, and switch the energy to a more positive place."

Nick obliged, finding it easier as he went along. He forgave family and friends, co-workers and rivals, and a collection of ex-girlfriends for offenses of varying degrees. As he disposed of the resentment, spite, and assorted grudges, the baggage slowly disappeared. He found it so liberating that he was surprised to see only one set of bags remained.

Nick recognized them at once. An old set of plaid suitcases stood side by side, three in all, each one worn and weathered by years of endless travel.

"These belonged to my father," he said.

"Then why are you still carrying them around?"

Nick stared at the bags. "My father left us when I was twelve. I'm not sure I can forgive him."

"You don't have to forgive everything today," explained the conductor. "There's a lot of weight here. Sometimes baggage comes in matching sets. Forgiving your father for abandoning you means forgiving him for other things as well ... for hurting your mother ... for making you wonder if it was somehow your fault."

Nick looked from bag to bag, the years of hurt connecting in his mind.

"We'll just leave them here," said the conductor. "You can forgive him when you're ready."

Nick sighed. "I'm sorry I can't get rid of everything."

"No one can get rid of it all, Nick. That's perfection. But you can clean out a whole lot of weight, and in doing so, begin dealing with the real baggage in your life." The conductor took a few steps toward the back of the train. "It's good to see that you're ready for forgiveness, though."

"Why is that?"

"That's how we're going to clear the caboose."

They exited the car and climbed into the caboose. The cargo was piled as high as it was in the previous car, but this time, it was all lined up on the left side.

"What's this stuff?"

"Mistakes. Misunderstandings. Things to ask forgiveness *for*."

"How am I going to ask forgiveness? There's no one here."

"Most people are willing to forgive our wrongdoings. Many of them are just waiting to be asked. We'll just do this car on the honor system." He picked up a pink bag with ballet slippers stitched on the side. "Recognize it?"

"It's my daughter's. I missed her dance recital, but I already apologized."

"Saying 'I'm sorry' gives *you* a chance to feel a little better. Asking forgiveness gives the opportunity to someone else. Didn't you feel good forgiving people in the last car?"

"I felt great."

"Then give Grace a chance to feel great. Ask her forgiveness so she can grant it and show you how much she cares."

"I'll do it," Nick said. "As soon as I see her."

"Excellent!" The conductor tossed the bag to the right wall of the car and picked up another.

"Wait a second," Nick said. "You just moved it from one side to the other. That's not getting rid of the weight, that's just rearranging it."

The young man gave Nick a serious look. "This is my job. Don't you think I know what I'm doing?"

"Sorry."

The conductor remained stationary, holding the bag and holding his stare.

Nick thought for a moment, then got the point. "I shouldn't have doubted you," he said. "Will you forgive me?"

The young man nodded. "Well, that takes care of that one!" He tossed the bag over his shoulder. "Ready to proceed?"

"Ready."

"Then let's take everything that's left and make it right."

The two men worked their way through the baggage. Nick vowed to ask forgiveness for thoughtless actions of the past, harsh words, and hurt feelings that had weighed heavily on his heart for years.

Minutes later, the remainder of bags had been moved to the right. The young man led Nick out of the caboose and into the car where they had been previously. Nick stood next to his father's bags, still on the floor where they had left them, and watched the conductor lean back through the door toward the caboose. The young man pulled a latch between the cars, causing the caboose to break away from the train and roll backward down a hill.

"Why did you do that?"

"You've let go of the guilt. You've released the regret."

"But it's still out there. The baggage hasn't really gone away."

"You haven't actually asked for forgiveness yet. Follow through with your promises and you'll never see that baggage again."

Nick watched the caboose disappear into the distance then noticed the conductor heading toward the front of the train. Nick followed him, pointing to his father's bags as he passed them.

"That's basically all the baggage we have left. We should be able to move again, right?"

The young man stopped as they entered a passenger car. "Actually, we should be moving now." He turned and looked at Nick. "Something's still weighing you down."

"I forgave others. I asked others for forgiveness. What's left?"

"Forgiving yourself."

"For what?"

"Your heaviest burden."

The young man pointed to Nick's heart. Nick reached up instinctively, his hands coming to rest on his coat pocket. The words and the realization came at once.

"My grandfather's watch."

Nick took out his grandfather's pocket watch slowly and stared at it. He offered the conductor an explanation. "He wanted to give it to me before he died. I didn't make it in time."

"Were you late on purpose?"

"No. But I shouldn't have been late at all."

"It was a bad choice. You can't hold on to the guilt forever."

"I should have been there, though. I should have heard what he wanted to say."

"Would you make the same mistake again?"

"Of course not."

"Then forgive yourself. There's nothing more precious than a second chance."

Nick looked at the watch in his open palm, unsure whether he could do what was asked.

"You have a long journey ahead of you. There are bridges to cross. Mountains to climb. Choose now to let it go." The young man reached out and closed Nick's fist around the watch. "You loved the man. He knows that. Do what you think he would want you to do."

Nick sighed and closed his eyes. He forgave himself for the mistake he had made and quietly let go of the guilt.

There was a sudden and startling jolt.

Released of its burden, the train rocketed forward, sending Nick stumbling back. He reached for support, lost hold of the watch, and shouted as it slipped from his grip. The conductor leaned forward and caught it inches above the ground. He lifted it to eye level, sighing with a sense of nostalgia.

"This is quite a watch."

Nick regained his balance, suddenly embarrassed by the watch's condition. "Some of the numbers are missing. Temporarily, anyway. It's kind of hard to explain, but it's helping me learn to make better use of my time."

"Maybe that's why your grandfather gave it to you."

"Why?"

"To help you learn how to spend your time." The young man placed the watch in Nick's hands, lingering a moment to look him in the eye. "Spend it wisely, Nicholas, spend it wisely. "

Nick's eyes widened as his grandfather's words registered. Scenery soared by as he stared back in silence, vaguely aware that the train was entering a city. The train's bell announced its arrival into the station and snapped Nick out of his silence.

"What now?" he asked, barely able to get the words out.

The conductor handed Nick a new ticket and motioned for him to look at it. "Chime Ten reminds you of the freeing power of forgiveness." Nick glanced down and saw the words to the chime.

⇒ CHIME 10 ⇐

TIME TO FORGIVE

I forgive others for hurting me.
I ask others for forgiveness for my wrongdoings.
I forgive myself for past failures.
After an act of forgiveness, I move on.

Nick saw the number ten appear on the watch. He held it up to show the conductor, but realized the young man had already walked away.

The train slowed, passing a series of pillars that sent shadows dancing through the car. The conductor glanced back occasionally as he made his way toward the rear of the train, his face seeming to age with every flash of light. By the time the train had stopped and the shadows had dwindled, he had vanished completely.

The door to Nick's car opened from the outside. Turning around quickly, he was surprised to see Max's head sticking in and looking around.

"There you are," the jaunty old man called. "I was starting to get worried."

Nick moved down the aisle and climbed off the train. "What are you doing here?"

"I was waiting for you," Max explained.

"How did you get here?"

"In style. Come on. I'll show you."

Max turned and headed away from the station. "I can't believe I beat the train."

"We got off to a rather slow start."

"Everything work out okay, though?"

"Everything worked out great."

"Told you it would."

"Sorry I doubted you."

Max smiled and snatched the ticket from Nick's hand. "You're forgiven."

Nick followed, replaying the trip in his head until a whistle and a yell announced the train's departure. He turned to watch it go, catching a fleeting glimpse of a familiar face, tipping his cap and waving goodbye.

Nick waved back, his heart feeling lighter than it had in years. He waited until the train had pulled away, then caught up to Max.

"I'm ready."

"Let's go then. The car's waiting."

"Waiting for what?"

"To take us to the party."

The ELEVENTH HOUR

As they stepped from the station, Nick was surprised by the coolness of the evening breeze. He was further surprised by the coolness of Max's car. He recognized the classic shape immediately.

"It's a '57 Chevy!"

"I know," answered Max, his voice swelling with pride. "I drove it here."

Nick ran his hands along the contours of the car. The copper-colored exterior, freshly polished, glistened in the moonlight. The retractable roof revealed vinyl seats and interior features in the same majestic color.

"This may be the most beautiful car I have ever seen."

"Ever driven one?"

"Not one like this."

Max met Nick at the front of the car. He dangled a key from his fingertips. "Take it."

"You're coming with me, right?"

"I'll be right beside you."

"And you're sure I can handle it?"

"You'll love it. It'll feel like you're flying."

"Let's do it then!"

Nick grabbed the key and hopped behind the wheel. Max climbed in beside him.

"Where to?"

"The Grand Hotel," Max said, pointing forward. "Straight down the strip. First hotel on your right."

Doors slammed, the engine roared, and the car darted forward like a comet in the night.

Nick relaxed behind the oversized steering wheel, breathing in the cool, fresh air. He streaked past neon lights, their colors flashing across his face. His heart continued to race as he pulled to a stop in the circular driveway of The Grand Hotel. The ride was short but exhilarating.

"Nice driving," Max said. "You didn't hit a single red light."

"Or pedestrian." Nick turned to Max and laughed. "That was some ride."

Max nodded and noticed a valet attendant approaching. He fished a gold coin out of his vest pocket and handed it to Nick. "Ask him to leave the car here. We won't be long."

"You don't want him to park it for you?"

"This car is a classic, Nick. I don't let just anyone drive it."

Nick did as he was asked and the valet followed suit. The men moved into the hotel, nodding to the doorman, and slipping into an elevator where a sleepy-eyed operator sat on a stool. He straightened up as they entered and addressed them politely.

"Which floor, please?"

Nick looked to Max. "The eleventh, right?" Max nodded. Nick turned to the operator and conveyed the message. "Eleven, please."

The operator pressed the button and the elevator shot up quickly. He sat back and sighed. "Everyone's headed for the eleventh floor tonight. Should be one heck of a party."

The operator stood as the elevator slowed down. "You guys made it just in time, too. The guest of honor is about to arrive."

"Guest of honor?" Nick asked. "Who's the guest of honor?"

Max pointed through the opening doors. "You are."

A red carpet ran from the edge of the elevator to a closed doorway in the distance. A sign outside the entrance read "Royal Suite." A banner hanging above it read "Welcome, Nick!"

Max placed a hand on Nick's back and guided him out of the elevator. As the doors shut behind him, Nick thought he heard the elevator operator laughing maniacally.

"I wasn't expecting this," Nick exclaimed nervously.

"Well, they're expecting you."

"Who?"

"Your guests."

Max pointed to a glass window in one of the doors. Nick leaned up and peeked through. A swing band was playing on a stage at the far side of the room. A gathering of people stood watching with their backs toward the door. Though Nick could see no faces, he was struck by the odd assortment of attire. There were tuxedos and gowns, gym shorts and T-shirts, and uniforms of several varieties. One guest even appeared to be wearing a hooded, black cloak.

Nick turned to speak to Max when he was surprised by an impatient voice calling out from the hallway.

"Can you move? You're blocking the door!"

Nick stepped aside as a gray-haired man in a white coat grunted and pushed his way into the room. Nick was about to comment on the man's demeanor when he was struck by a realization.

"Wait a second. I think I know that guy!" Nick peeked through the window for a second look. "That was Dr. Wesley! He pulled my teeth when I needed braces."

"He's a dentist?"

"He's a demon! He tortured me for years. I've feared dentists ever since. Why is he here?"

"I invited him."

"You invited my dentist? What's the chime? Time for a check-up?" Nick watched as the man shook hands with the guest in the black cloak. "I told you he was a demon. Look. He's shaking hands with the guy dressed as Death!"

Max leaned over and looked. "That guy's not dressed as Death." He stepped back and stared at Nick. "That guy *is* Death."

"You invited Death?"

"You don't have to invite Death, Nick. He just sort of shows up."

"So Death is in there. And my dentist. Who else?"

Max pointed through the window. "A bald man, a poor man, a lonely man whose wife has left him ... "

Nick laughed uncomfortably. "Combine those guys together and you've got all my nightmares rolled into one."

Max turned to Nick and gave him a look. Nick shook his head and took a step back. "Wait a second.

This isn't a fear thing, is it?"

Max nodded. "I'm afraid so."

"*You're* afraid?" Nick stole another peep through the window. "You've brought everything I've feared my entire life into one room." He looked back to Max. "I can't do it. There's no way I can go in there."

"It's the eleventh hour, Nick. Go one-on-one with your fears. You can handle this." Max pushed the door open and pointed in. "Time to be brave."

Music drifted from the room. Max drifted in. Nick followed slowly, his eyes darting ahead to gauge what was going on. He was trying to use Max as a shield when a young woman with big blond hair and a bigger voice bounded in between them.

"Nicky!" she squealed, squeezing him in an uninvited hug. "Randy told me why you haven't called." She rifled through her purse, popped a piece of bubble gum into her mouth, then scribbled on the wrapper. "Here's my number. Again." She waved her finger and frowned like a mother scolding a child. "And don't lose it this time." She blew a bubble, bursting it with her finger. "Gotta run now. But call me, okay?" She moved on without waiting for a reply, waving as she made her way through the crowd.

Nick waved back with the hand that held the wrapper. He dropped it onto the tray of a passing waiter and turned to Max.

"Suzie Hanford," he explained. "Had a blind date with her my second year of college. She scared the daylights out of me."

"And you never called her?"

"I called her lots of things. I just never went out with her again." Nick looked around the room, worried about who he would see next. "You know, you've been working really hard and I'm not really in a 'party' kind of mood, so what do you say we call it quits and punch out early?"

Max laughed. "We can't do that. But, speaking of punching out … do remember the name 'Archie McFarland'?"

"Remember the name? I remember the fist. He used to beat me up in grammar school. He's big. He's mean. He's … "

"behind you."

Nick was struck with a sudden sense of shock. He pictured a full-grown Archie towering over him and glowering down. He looked to Max for support.

"Be brave," Max whispered. "Draw forth courage. Face your fear."

Nick took a deep breath and turned slowly, resolving to look his tormentor in the eye. He had to look down to do so.

Archie stood before him looking exactly as he had in grade school: his fists clenched, his face scrunched in full tough-guy mode, his head no higher than Nick's stomach. Nick let out a laugh before realizing he'd done so.

"Something funny?" Archie asked, attempting to sound threatening.

Nick stifled a laugh and answered, "No."

"Good." Archie pounded his fist into his hand then pointed his finger in Nick's face. "Cause I'd hate to see what would happen to you if I thought you were laughing at me."

Archie glared at Nick for a moment then turned away. The squat bully grabbed a handful of snacks from a banquet table, shoved them in his pocket, and pushed his way through the crowd.

Nick laughed again and turned to Max. "That was pretty easy."

"Sometimes what we fear isn't as scary as we think. Why aren't you afraid of Archie anymore?"

"I've matured."

"You would never have known that if you hadn't faced him." Max began walking and indicated for Nick to follow. "It's like that for most of us, Nick. Something frightens us early on – in childhood, in a relationship, in business – and we go out of our way to avoid it. In the meantime, we grow. We get stronger, wiser, more skilled. So much so that we could easily conquer our fears if we could just convince ourselves to face them."

Nick took a deep breath. "I'm ready. What's next?"

Max pointed to a small door on a distant wall. "Just step out onto that balcony over there."

"Is this a height thing? Cause I think we covered that with the whole airplane on the mountain adventure."

"It's not about height. Something's waiting for you out there."

Nick took a step toward the balcony and stopped. "Something's waiting for me?"

Max nodded. "Sounds ominous, doesn't it?"

Nick glanced around the room to see if any of the recognizable guests had slipped out ahead of him. Death was busy dancing, employing his sickle as a limbo stick and encouraging others to duck underneath. Dr. Wesley was trying to escape the grasp of Suzie Hanford, who had her mouth open, as usual, seeking advice on how to care for her remarkably large set of teeth. Little Archie McFarland hid behind a table, snickering as he pelted peanuts at members of the band.

Nick peeked through a window and saw a shadowy figure pacing near the edge of the balcony. The height and hairline seemed so familiar that his first thought was he was looking at an older version of himself. When the figure turned and paced toward the window, Nick got a closer look.

"It's my father."

"He's waiting to talk with you."

"I'm not sure I can do this."

"It's your choice. Part of bravery is making the right decision, especially when it's a difficult one."

"Why is he here? What does he want?" Nick asked, speaking more to himself than to Max.

"You won't know until you face him."

Nick placed a hand on the door, but held himself back. Max noticed the indecision and offered additional advice.

"Just be honest with yourself, Nick. Have you wanted to talk to him?"

"Talk to him? Yes. Forgive him? No."

"Then tell him that."

Nick nodded. He took a deep breath and opened the door. A brisk night breeze greeted him as he stepped onto the balcony. His father turned toward him, cautiously extending a hand he addressed him in a faintly familiar tone.

"It's good to see you, Nick."

Nick moved away slightly. "Why are you here?"

"I ... wanted to see you, to talk to you."

"It's been thirty years, Dad. You've had plenty of opportunity."

"That's not fair. You could have called me, too, you know. I'm not that hard to find."

"So it's my fault?"

"No." The man answered quickly, obviously upset with himself for his previous response. He ran a hand through his thinning hair and started to shake, perhaps from nervousness, perhaps from the cold, perhaps from a combination of both. "It's my fault, Nick. I know that. I should have called you. I started to call you a hundred times. I just never got the nerve."

"You had a lot of nerve," Nick said, his defenses still up. "How could you bail out on Mom and me like that?"

"I got scared. Restless. A family was just so much more responsibility than I was ready for. I was a workaholic. I wanted success. There was just so little time. I should have found a way to make it work."

"Why didn't you?"

"I wasn't brave. I just left. Told myself it was to

look for new opportunities. Told myself I'd travel, earn a better living, then come back. I almost did, too. Several times. I just kept thinking that I could do a little better. After a while, it just seemed easier to stay away."

"It wasn't easier for us." Nick moved closer to his father, sitting in a chair at a table. "I don't understand how you could just leave people you cared about. You never even said good-bye. You could have at least let me know you were going."

"I tried to, once," his father said, sitting across from him. "I don't suppose you remember what I told you about the shark."

Nick bowed his head, the meaning of his father's words becoming clear as he spoke them aloud. "He has to keep moving to survive."

"That was me, I guess. The shark. I had to move in order to live. Only, it isn't much of a life."

"No," Nick said, looking his father in the eye for the first time, "it isn't."

The two men stared at each other without speaking, Nick's father envisioning the boy he left behind, Nick envisioning the man he would become if he failed to slow down. Nick broke the silence without breaking eye contact.

"I can't forgive you for leaving us."

"I don't expect you to."

"I understand the desire to succeed, though. I'm afraid I inherited quite a bit of that."

"There's nothing wrong with wanting success, Nick. There are just different ways you can choose to measure it. I chose poorly. I lost sight of what was really important and lost the things that mattered most. I just wanted to explain that, and to tell you how much I regret it."

"I regret it, too, Dad." Nick cleared his throat as emotion filled the moment. "I missed you. Mom missed you."

"And I … missed out."

The man leaned his elbows on the table and lowered his head into his hands. Nick stood, wanting to comfort his father and confront him at the same time. He hesitated a moment, then placed a hand on his father's shoulder.

"I will call you, Dad. We can't make up for lost time, but there's no need to lose anymore."

The man looked up, his face revealing the faintest trace of a smile. "I look forward to it, son. I really do."

Nick moved slowly to the door. He opened it halfway then looked back. "I look forward to it, too." Nick turned to move off the balcony, bumping into Max in the doorway.

"I'm proud of you, Nick. That took a lot of courage."

"Facing my father?"

"Deciding to call him. Resolving to take the first step."

"He came to see me. He took the first step."

"Did he?" Max's tone was confusing. Nick looked back and saw an empty balcony.

"He wasn't here?"

Max pointed a finger and touched Nick's heart. "He was here."

"So, none of that was real?"

"The emotions were. You've been thinking of calling your father for years. You've just been afraid. Now that you've envisioned what can happen, you're ready to do it for real."

"What if it doesn't go so well?"

"What if it goes better?"

Nick contemplated Max's words. Max led him across the room, pointing to guests as they passed.

"People avoid things because of fear, Nick. They don't give up bad habits because they are afraid they won't be able to cope. They shun new challenges because they are afraid of failure. They avoid relationships because they are afraid of getting hurt."

"And they miss out." Nick sighed and made a resolution. "I'm going to call my dad. I'm going to see what happens. I'm going to stop avoiding things just because I'm afraid."

"That's my boy." Max handed Nick an empty plate and pointed him to a buffet table. "Grab a bite to eat now. I'll be right back."

Nick looked at the table. The display of food caught his eye and turned his stomach. A serving of escargot perched near a large anchovy pizza. A bowl of broccoli sat to the side. He smirked and took a small serving of each.

Taking tentative bites, he turned and tried to find Max in the crowd. His eyes drifted past faces that were slowly becoming familiar: a college professor, a former colleague, the father of an old friend. He flashed over moments he had yielded to fear, wondering what he had missed by not standing up for beliefs, by not taking risks, by not pursuing opportunities.

A chime sounded. Nick's thoughts faded as his eyes fell upon Max. Max stood commandingly at the microphone at the front of the stage, tapping a silver spoon on the side of a crystal glass.

"Now that I have everyone's attention, let's give one more round of applause for our guest of honor and see if we can get him up here!"

Nick swallowed hard. A snail slid down his throat. The crowd cheered as he set down his plate and made his way across the room.

"Speech! Speech!"

Nick stepped up on the stage and addressed Max quietly.

"I can't make a speech."

"Because you're not brave?" Max asked.

"Because I'm not prepared. What am I supposed to say?"

"Chime Eleven reminds you to be brave, and go one-on-one with your fears. Try this."

Max drew a paper napkin from his coat pocket and handed it to Nick. Nick glanced at the writing on the napkin, peered out at the crowd, and came face-to-face with all of his fears at once. He cleared his throat and addressed them.

⋙ CHIME 11 ⋘

TIME TO BE BRAVE

*I am courageous during the
challenges in my life.*

*I make the right decisions in
difficult situations.*

I adventure into healthy, new experiences.

I am not afraid to make mistakes.

The crowd applauded.

Nick pulled out his watch and saw the number eleven materialize. He raised his hand and showed the crowd.

"My chime is up, folks," he said, smiling. "Looks like I'd better be on my way." He started off, then leaned back to the microphone. "Thanks for coming, everyone. Try the snails before you go."

Max whispered a question as Nick exited the stage. "What would you do if you were brave today?"

Nick smiled coyly. "I'd adventure into new experiences."

"Where do you want to go?"

"How about the final chime?"

"Excellent decision."

Nick followed Max to an open window. Max turned to Nick and pointed to a couch against the wall. "Hand me a throw pillow, will you?"

Nick did as he was asked. "What are you going to

do with it?"

"Throw it, of course."

Max tossed the pillow, spinning it out into the evening sky. Nick leaned over to watch it fall and was surprised by what he saw. Instead of appearing smaller as it fell into the distance, the pillow actually grew larger. It drifted downward, expanding magically and landing softly in the center of the circular driveway at the hotel's entrance.

Max gave a nod of approval and began to climb onto the window ledge. "Give me a hand, will you?"

"You're not going to jump, are you?"

"Of course not. *We're* going to jump." He turned and extended a hand toward Nick. "Climb up, Nick. Come to the edge."

Knowing Max had never led him wrong, Nick stepped up nervously. He glanced down at the giant pillow waiting like a crash cushion eleven stories below.

"Hand me your watch."

Nick offered it hesitantly, and then stared in horror as Max took the timepiece and casually flung it out the window.

"Hey! I need that!"

"Go get it then."

"You're coming with me, right?"

"I'll be right beside you."

"And you're sure I can handle it?"

"You'll love it. It'll feel like you're flying."

Their hands clasped. Their knees bent. Their hearts soared.

"Ready, set ... "

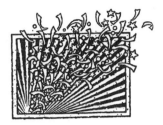

Happy New Year

"Go!"

They jumped. Acceleration led to exhilaration and the air filled with a strange haze. They cheered joyously, the sounds of a working clock rattling in their ears.

As the men sailed downward, phantom images of numbers began passing before their eyes. The numbers increased in value, spiraling around them, until a final "11" emerged from the mist.

Nick and Max landed together, feet-first on a

long, black, metal plank. It gave a bit upon impact, cushioning their fall, bobbing like a diving board before settling back into position.

Nick gave Max a look of disbelief and began to walk along the plank. There were two others beside the one on which they had landed. The additional planks, slightly different in size and shape, stretched out before them like long steps in a circular staircase. A majestic number one was painted on the gleaming, white floor to the right of the planks. An equally impressive number eleven was painted to the left.

Max was the first to speak. "Trying to figure out where we are?"

Nick turned toward his friend. "Actually, I was trying to figure out where my watch went."

Max laughed. "Take a *minute* to look for it. Don't get yourself all *wound up*. You'll figure it out any *second*."

Nick gave Max a quizzical look then surveyed his surroundings. A round room, gold walls, a dome of glass ...

He smiled. "Are we ... inside it?"

"Bravo!"

Nick was amazed. His mind was spinning. His body was doing the same.

"How did this happen? Did the watch get bigger or did we get smaller? And how could we fall through the domed roof?"

Max raised a hand to relax him. "How we got here isn't important." Max smiled and hopped down to the second plank. "On the other hand," he laughed, "why we're here matters a lot."

"So tell me."

"We're here so you can view the chimes from a new perspective." Max moved to a small, raised platform where the three planks seemed to meet. He beckoned Nick. "You should see the view from here."

Nick joined Max at the center pin and saw the planks for what they really were: three frozen hands fanning out at slight increments. The one Nick had walked on, the second hand, stood a tick away from the empty twelve spot. Max's plank, the minute hand, stood a bit closer. The third, the hour hand, was just about there.

Nick pointed to the position of high noon. "The

twelve is still missing."

"That's what we're here for." Max gestured to the numbers that surrounded them. "Do you see where you're standing, Nick? You're right in the center of all the chimes. Chime Twelve will teach you how to connect the chimes to the wisdom inside you."

"What do I do next?"

"Look over the chimes. Think about your strengths and your challenges. You're already a sage in some areas, but you're a struggler in others." Max raised his arm and the second-hand glided to the number one. "Time to Yourself," Max continued. "This one is a challenge for you, but you're strong in Chime Eleven, Time to be Brave."

The second hand moved again as if commanded by Max's words. It swung swiftly and smoothly around the face of the clock until it reached the eleven.

"You did a great job of facing your fears. Why not put your bravery toward Chime One? Take bold steps to secure time for yourself. Your wisdom will grow and positive life experiences will grow with it."

Nick nodded as the words sunk in. The hand started moving slowly. Max pointed to the numbers as it passed over them.

"Can you apply your fearlessness to other chimes? Chime Three: Time to Give? Chime Four: Time to Relate?"

"I could definitely use some help with relationships."

"Invest some bravery then. Use the power from a chime you are mastering to strengthen a chime that proves more challenging."

The second hand came to rest at high noon. Nick smiled at Max.

"I think I got it."

Max smiled back. "Why don't you to take her for a spin then?"

Nick thought for a moment, glanced at the numbers surrounding him, then nodded. He pointed to the number two and the second hand followed.

"I can be Positive," he said, turning and pointing to the number five, "when it's ... Time to Learn."

The hand swept into place, stopping at the number five. Nick grinned and pointed again. The second hand wheeled along with his words. "I can take Time to Play so I can have more Time to be in the Moment. I can work at being more giving!"

"Well done." Max waved his arm and the second hand swung to the vacant position atop the watch. He stepped onto it and gestured for Nick to follow. "You're doing great, Nick. You're almost there."

Max paused at the edge of the hand and pointed down. The thin outline of the number twelve was now visible. Nick looked to Max, eager to hear more.

"The Twelfth Chime is the one that completes the circle. It connects all of the Chimes together. When you take the power of the Twelfth Chime and apply it to the others, they will all lift. And you'll be on track to live a thousand years."

Nick nodded anxiously. "So what is the Twelfth Chime?"

"Chime Twelve: Time to Reset."

"Reset?"

"It's the key to using your chimes wisely. You choose to reset your mind and recalibrate all of the areas of your life."

Max snapped his finger. The second hand moved, taking the men around the face of the clock. Max pointed to the numbers as they traveled over them.

"The hands of the clock all return to twelve before they go round again. As time advances, the clock resets. You have to reset as well. No matter how big your successes or failures may be, there is always a time to reset."

"Why would I want to reset if I'm successful?"

"Think about it, Nick. How many people do you know who are still celebrating successes they had years ago?"

"Too many."

"Exactly. Real winners don't only reset after life's setbacks. They quickly reset after successes as well."

Nick folded his arms and thought about how self-satisfied he'd become in certain areas of his life: taking people he loved for granted, assuming he knew everything about success.

"Celebrate your accomplishments for a day," Max offered. "Celebrate for a week. Celebrate for a month, if you must. BUT GET OVER IT!"

Max's words echoed off the domed ceiling. The second hand stopped again at the number twelve, slightly more visible than it had been moments before. Max led Nick back to the center pin, reached into his coat, and pulled out a round, apple-red alarm clock.

Nick looked at the object, finding it strangely familiar. "Where did you get this?"

Max shrugged. "Your past."

Nick examined the dents and the details of the clock until it struck him. "Wait a second. This used to sit next to my bed when I was a kid."

"It looks a little beat up."

Nick smirked. "I may have smashed it a few times."

"Why? Because it kept waking you up?"

"No. Because it never woke me up! I could never get it to work right."

"The clock was trying to teach you a lesson, Nick: the importance of rest. Sleep is your body's way of resetting itself. It's important to sleep well."

"I used to sleep well. I usually slept late. I kept forgetting to wind that stupid thing."

"What happened when you didn't wind it?"

"It stopped working. Caused all kinds of trouble."

"Another lesson it was teaching you. This alarm clock is like your life. If you want it to work properly, it has to be reset. The faster you reset, the more positive life experience you will have."

"The more positive life experience, the greater your Sage Age."

Max patted his companion on the back and placed the clock on the ground. "Nick, my boy, it looks like you're finally making the right connections."

"So, what now?"

"Now?" Max raised his eyebrows playfully. "I make a few connections of my own!"

Reaching into his pockets, Max began digging out the slips of paper that Nick had earned throughout his adventures: the sales receipt from the auction in Chime One, the check from the diner in Chime Six, the napkin with his speech in Chime Eleven.

Max pressed the papers into a pile. Whirling his hands in a flurry of motion, he began folding them in every conceivable direction. He turned them inside out, twisted them right side up, and twirled them backwards, transforming them with his fingertips.

Nick watched in wonder as an array of shapes flashed before his eyes: a paper suit, a ship, an airplane. Origami images from each of the Twelve Chimes emerged and dissolved like magic until a thunderous clap of Max's hands collapsed them into his palms. Unable to see the papers, Nick looked up into Max's eyes. Max stared back and spoke.

"Learn the Twelve Chimes. Memorize them. Live by them."

He raised an eyebrow then opened his hands to reveal the result of his work. A tiny stack of papers sat folded in the center of his palm. "This is a little something I've been working on. Just a prototype really. Let me know what you think." Max lifted the tiny papers, tugged on the corners, and stretched them into a full-sized calendar. He presented it with a flourish. "It's a Twelve Chime Calendar," he explained. "My own design. A separate chime for each month."

Nick took the calendar in his hands. There were

no wrinkles. No torn edges. No sign that it had ever been anything but a calendar. He turned the pages and admired the design. Imagery from each of the lessons adorned the pages. Written words recounted the essential message of each chime.

Nick was about to compliment Max on his work when he paused, confused. He looked up at Max and spoke tentatively. "I ... think you've made a mistake."

"What do you mean?"

Nick handed the calendar back to Max. "Look at the dates."

Max opened to the first page and read. "January 1. Happy New Year." He looked up and shrugged.

"Keep going."

Max sighed and read again. "January 2. Happy New Year."

Nick smiled. "See?"

Max smiled back. "No."

Nick was baffled. He took the calendar and read. "January 3. Happy New Year." He flipped the calendar and pointed to a random date. "June 20. Happy New Year." Getting no reaction from Max, he turned and pointed for a third time. "October 31. Halloween. Happy New Year."

"I don't understand your point."

"You've put the words 'Happy New Year' on every date! How can every day be New Year's Day?"

Max took the calendar back and pointed to its pages. "It all depends on how you look at things, Nick. There is a full year between this January first and the next, just as there is a full year between one birthday and the one that follows. The fact is, there is a new year every single day. Do you understand?"

"I guess. I mean, I understand the concept, but what's the point of putting it on the calendar?"

"New Year's Day is an important day for a lot of people. It is a time when people resolve to cut off the past and begin fresh, a kind of rebirth. More people reset on New Year's Day than on any other day of the year. You don't have to wait for the first of January, though. You can reset anytime, anyplace, anywhere."

"But how do I know when to do it?"

"There are 365 days to choose from." Max flipped the pages. The months flashed like cards being shuffled. "But you have to choose. Sooner or later, the days run out." The final page flipped by and the calendar vanished in thin air.

Nick's eyes went wide. "What happened? Why'd you get rid of it? Didn't you like it?"

"I liked it a lot, but I think I can do better. It won't be the first time I decided to begin anew."

Max walked in a circle around Nick. His mind raced into the past.

"When I started my job as the Time Being, I faced all sorts of challenges. Calibrating the world's clocks. Synchronizing time zones. Keeping track of the grains of sand. I remember telling myself, 'I'll do better next year.' But, then I thought, 'Why wait till the end of the year?' If I want to change, I'll change sooner – 'I'll do better next season!' Then I thought, 'Why the end of the season? How 'bout the end of the month? The end of the week? The end of the day? How about the end of the hour? The minute? How about right now?'"

The apple-red alarm clock went off in a racket of ringing bells. Max took a running start and punted the clock straight up. The dome above them shattered.

"HAPPY NEW YEAR!"

Nick cringed as the glass cascaded downward, but joined Max in a cheer as it transformed into a colorful shower of confetti. "Auld Lange Syne" reverberated through the room. Max raised his voice over the clamor.

"Chime Twelve reminds you to reset. The faster you reset after failure and success, the more you will make of your time. Get rest. Cut off from the past and begin anew. Happy New Year today!"

In the midst of the festivity, Nick was overcome by a joyous sense of peace. He looked to the edge of the enormous hands and watched the number twelve return to its rightful place. It appeared in its entirety, connecting the chimes and completing the circle.

The confetti began to rain thicker, falling in a glittering downpour. Max plucked a piece of paper from the air and handed it to Nick to read:

⤙ CHIME 12 ⤚

TIME TO RESET

I reset quickly after failure and begin again.

*I reset quickly after success and
reach for higher aspirations.*

I sleep well and get enough rest.

I cherish each day.

Max clasped Nick's shoulder.

"Time to reset," he whispered. "Time to go home."

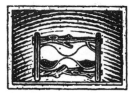

Back to the Hourglass

MAX MOVED FORWARD, DISAPPEARING INTO THE storm of confetti. The paper swirled around him in vibrant colors, making it look as though he were walking through a kaleidoscope.

Nick followed blindly, unable to make out the form of Max in front of him, yet confident he was on the right course.

After a few moments, the confetti began to dissipate and a doorway appeared in the distance. Max slipped inside and Nick followed behind him. They had returned to the place where their adventure had begun. They had returned to the back room of Max's shop.

"We made it!"

"We did, indeed," Max said. "We did, indeed."

Max reached forward and blew a small pile of confetti off his palm. In a burst of breath and color, Nick's watch reappeared in its original size, resting safely in Max's outstretched hand.

"Your Twelve Chimes, sir."

Nick smiled at Max's magic. He took the watch and sat down at the table to examine it. "The hands aren't moving yet," he said, "but the numbers are all back."

Max nodded. "You've earned them. Hopefully, they have more meaning to you now."

"They do." Nick looked to his friend with deep appreciation. "I don't know how to thank you."

"You can promise me something."

"Anything."

"Ponder and practice the Twelve Chimes everyday. Remember, being wise is not just knowing wisdom, but living it. Whenever you see those numbers, on your watch, on a clock, anywhere, I want you to remember to live your life by the wisdom of the chimes."

"I will. You can count on it."

"Good. Speaking of counting, I have a little math for you." Max reached into his vest, removed his calculator, and punched a few buttons. He set it on the table and slid it toward Nick. "It's your up-to-date Sage Age. I factored in what you've done, what you've experienced, what you've learned."

Nick read the number and raised an eyebrow. "Not too shabby." He did some quick math in his head, then looked up to Max. "I'm never going to make it, though."

"Make what?"

"Make it to a thousand. I'm forty-three already. I started too late."

"It's never too late, Nick. Use the chimes to live your life to the fullest. If you don't make it to a thousand in your lifetime, your legacy will continue your work."

"My legacy?"

"What you teach others. How you lead by example.

Think about your grandfather. He left a while ago, but his legacy lives on in you. Your legacy will live on, too, in Alicia, in Grace ... in grandchildren yet to be born."

"I guess I had better get started."

"It'll be easy for you, Nick. You've got the desire. You've discovered where you are. You know your destination and the direction you want to take. All you need is the determination to make it happen."

"I've got it. Don't you worry."

"I'm not worried. Not at all. Not anymore."

Max removed his coat and headed for the hook on the wall. As he reached to hang it up, something fell from a pocket, gliding softly to the floor by Nick's feet. Nick picked it up, smiling in surprise.

"It's our picture. The one from Mosaic Park."

Max leaned in to admire it. "We look great."

"I thought you folded this into the calendar."

"I never fold the photographs. I save them for the scrapbook." Max reached over to a shelf, removed a large, leather-bound album, and set it on the table "Call me sentimental, but I'm a softie when it comes to souvenirs."

"You've got other photographs?"

"You're not the first to take this journey, Nick. Nor will you be the last."

Max opened the worn leather cover and thumbed slowly through the thick, black pages.

There were several photos glued to each sheet. As Max took a moment to linger over the pictures, Nick moved closer, to marvel at Max's collection.

The early pages featured antique photographs in faded sepia tone. The next section contained snapshots in crisp black-and-white. A third section was comprised of contemporary pictures in vivid color. Though the style of the photos varied, the images captured were remarkably similar. Each one showed Max and a companion, standing side-by-side, smiling brightly in the midst of Mosaic Park.

Nick found several of the faces instantly familiar: Phil and Ann Thropy. Captain Kip. Little Sophie from the playground.

"All these people learned from you?"

"And you learned from them." Max took Nick's

photo and glued it to a page. "When you're ready to share the wisdom of the chimes, others, young and old, will learn from you."

"I'm ready now."

Max smiled and pointed to the hourglass. "I'd better put you back in there, then." He closed the scrapbook and began patting the pockets of his vest. "I just need to find you first." He scratched his beard as if he were deep in thought. "I know I put you somewhere."

Nick's eyes widened as he waited uncomfortably. Max checked the pockets of the coat he had hung on the wall, then bowed his head in defeat. Nick was about to do the same when Max looked up and laughed.

"Gotcha!"

Nick's sigh turned slowly to a smile. "I can't believe you did that to me."

"I can't believe you fell for it."

Max reached under his collar and removed the locket he wore around his neck. He opened it slowly, releasing a golden light that radiated from within. He picked up his tiny tweezers and plucked something from the center of the locket.

"Your grain of sand. Safe and sound."

Nick smiled. Max smiled back. Neither man moved.

"Aren't you going to put me back?"

"Not while you're watching."

"So, I'm not allowed to see where I am in the whole scheme of things?" Nick moved to the hourglass and looked inside. "Can you give me a hint? How close am I to ... the other side?"

Max avoided the question. He looked from the tweezers to the hourglass then smiled slyly. "If you make me hold this too long, I might drop it. There's a lot of dust on the floor. I'd hate to see you lost forever."

"Fine," Nick said. "You don't have to tell me. It's not how long I live that's important. It's how wisely I live."

"I'm glad to see I wasn't wasting time with you."

"There will be no more wasted time with me. I promise."

Max reached out to shake Nick's hand. Nick moved forward, deciding at the last moment to give him a hug instead. "Thank you," he whispered. "For everything."

The embrace continued silently. When Nick found himself unable to come up with words, he squeezed tighter. Max came up with words of his own.

"Yeeouch!"

Max staggered back, grimacing and gripping his vest.

Nick tensed, unsure how to respond. "What is it?"

"It's a big one!"

"A heart attack?"

"A fish hook!"

Max reached his right hand into his breast pocket and began fidgeting around. He steadied his left hand so as not to drop the tweezers.

Nick's concern was all for his friend. "Are you okay?"

"I'm fine. Nothing serious." Max pulled out a plastic fish with several dangling hooks. "I call this one Big Ben." He set it on the counter and smiled. "Nothing I hate more than a painful goodbye."

They laughed for a moment until Nick extended his hand. Max looked at it suspiciously.

"You're not going to lure me into another hug, are you?"

Nick shook his head. "I'm not going to hug you into another lure either."

They shook hands warmly, saying more with their eyes than they could have with words. Nick broke away first and moved toward the curtain that led from the room.

"Well," he said, looking back, "I've got a lot to do. I'd better run."

"Enjoy your dash."

Nick nodded and turned around. He made it halfway to the front door before he returned.

"Um, everything's still frozen out there. You never put me back."

"You never gave me the chance." Max held out the tweezers and headed for the hourglass. "Just stand there and close your eyes," he instructed. "I'll make everything the same as it was before."

Nick closed his eyes and smiled. "It'll never be the same as it was before. Not for me, anyway."

There was a faint squeak as Max opened the glass

door in the side of the hourglass. Although Nick was tempted to peek and see where he was being placed, he kept his eyes closed, breathless with anticipation.

"Viva mille anni," he heard Max whisper. "Live a thousand years."

A SECOND CHANCE

THE SUDDEN STIR OF VOICES MADE NICK THINK that a group of visitors had suddenly stumbled into the back of Max's shop. He opened his eyes and realized that it was he who had done the traveling.

He had returned to the street-side café. He looked at his watch. The second hand moved a single tick, joining the others to indicate high noon.

With one swift glance, Nick took in everything: the waitress pouring water behind him, the woman and man ending their passionate kiss, the noisy grind of the city traffic – a welcome sound for the first time.

A town clock played loudly in the distance. Recalling the promise he had made to Max, Nick listened and said the Chimes in his head as the bells chimed high noon.

CHIME ONE: *Time to Yourself*
CHIME TWO: *Time to Be Positive*
CHIME THREE: *Time to Give*
CHIME FOUR: *Time for Relationships*
CHIME FIVE: *Time to Learn*
CHIME SIX: *Time in the Moment*
CHIME SEVEN: *Time to Dream*
CHIME EIGHT: *Time to Play*
CHIME NINE: *Time to Work*
CHIME TEN: *Time to Forgive*
CHIME ELEVEN: *Time to Be Brave*
CHIME TWELVE: *Time to Reset*

Nick smiled at his success. He glanced at his watch to make sure it was working. With the sudden arrival of his client, he remembered that he was working, too. He slipped the watch into his pocket and greeted the man with a firm handshake.

"Nice to finally meet you in person," Nick said, gesturing toward a chair. "Please have a seat."

Nick watched closely as the man sat. The quick observation was a reflex maneuver, a time-tested method of sizing up his client in order to gain an edge. This time, however, Nick was no longer looking for the upper hand. He was searching for the kid inside.

"I brought the proposal you sent," the man explained. "Should we order something first or shall we get right down to business?"

Nick leaned forward and flashed a grin. "You know what I could go for right now? A milkshake."

"A milkshake?"

Nick enjoyed the surprise he saw on his client's face. "You want one? My treat."

The client hesitated, trying to guess whether Nick's question was some sort of joke. He watched Nick signal for the waitress. "You're serious, aren't you?"

"I'm ordering a milkshake in the middle of a business meeting. How serious can I be?" He looked at his client with mock urgency. "The waitress is on her way. I'm going to need a decision."

The man shrugged and smiled. "Make mine chocolate."

Nick smiled back and turned to the waitress as she reached the table. "Two chocolate shakes, please."

The waitress gave the men an odd look and walked away.

"Did you see her face?" Nick asked. "Guess we don't look like the milkshake types."

The client laughed. "You know, I don't think I've had a milkshake in twenty years."

"How old are you?"

"Fifty-seven. You?"

"Forty-three. But I'm hoping to make it to a thousand."

"What?"

"Seriously. My grandfather made it to 525. Let me show you something."

Nick grabbed a pen and pad and began sketching a tombstone. "When you die," he said, sliding it over for his client to see, "they'll carve two dates on your tombstone. Two dates divided by a dash. Which is the most important carving?"

Less than two hours later, Nick felt a great sense of accomplishment. He had enjoyed a milkshake, closed a deal, and shared the secrets of the Twelve Chimes. He had even managed to hail a cab to take him home.

Settling into the back of the taxi, he noted the traffic ahead. He set his notebook on his lap, knowing the long ride would give him plenty of time to make some lists. He began with his immediate goals: flowers for his wife, forgiveness from his daughter, a phone call to his father.

He was about to begin a list of long-term plans when he noticed the clock shop outside his window. Asking the driver to pull over, he hopped out, hoping for another moment with Max. He hurried to the door, frowning when he found it locked.

"You looking for The Timekeeper?"

Nick turned toward the voice. The young man at the newspaper stand left his post and wandered over. "You just missed him."

"You know where he went?"

"Vacation. Just shut down the shop on a whim. Asked me to let people know if they came by."

"Did he say when he was coming back?"

"He wasn't sure. Said something about 'resetting.' Whatever that means."

Nick smiled. "I wonder where he went."

"Some island," the young man said, heading back to the stand. "Said he was going to do a little fishing … spend some time with a lady friend. That'll be fun for the time being."

Nick nodded, turning to the window. "It sure will." He touched his hand to the glass and whispered. "Happy New Year, old timer. Happy New Year."

Climbing back into the taxi, Nick took a last look at the shop, smiling at what he saw in the window. The clocks, each one with hands reading ten minutes until two, seemed to be smiling back.

"Thanks for waiting," he said to the driver. "We can head home now."

The driver nodded, merging slowly onto the street. "Traffic's pretty bad," he called back. "It's going to take a while."

"Not a problem," Nick answered. "I'm in no hurry."

He took his grandfather's watch in his hands and ran his fingers around its face. He paused at each number, recalling the chimes and looking forward to the rewards they would bring. When he completed the circle, he closed his eyes and conjured a vision.

A single fin cut swiftly through the water, gaining momentum as it shot through the surface. In an instant, it was airborne. A dolphin this time, instead of a shark, it soared skyward as if it believed it could fly. It laughed freely as it reached its peak, flipped forward, and dove back into the sea.

Nick watched the ripples travel through the water. He envisioned his life moving with them, expanding farther and wider than he had ever imagined possible. Opening his eyes, he saw his face reflected in the crystal of his grandfather's watch. The smooth, round surface of the watch was like a ripple frozen in time – a wondrous circle connecting all the chimes.

Nick flashed himself a smile, sat back, and knew he was going to enjoy the rest of the ride.

ABOUT THE AUTHOR

Giovanni Livera has spent much of *his* precious time teaching people how to reach their full potential. For years, he has wowed Fortune 500 audiences with his powerful "Anything Is Possible" message, reinforced by magical feats of possibility.

Now, he inspires audiences worldwide to create richer, more meaningful lives. By teaching people how to "Live A Thousand Years," he helps them gain a new appreciation of time and encourages them to grow in astonishing new ways.

Giovanni's presentations reverberate with goodwill, love and integrity, thanks to his boundless energy and one-of-a-kind communication style. His amazing acts of magic, audience involvement, and storytelling teach us how to get the most out of life and create our own personal legacies. He stimulates our sense of wonder and enthusiasm as he "lifts the audience up and brings the house down!"

Giovanni, who performed his first magic show at the age of seven, is an International Brotherhood of Magicians World Champion and has been nominated to the Speakers Hall of Fame. He is living a thousand years in Orlando, Florida, with his wife and two daughters.

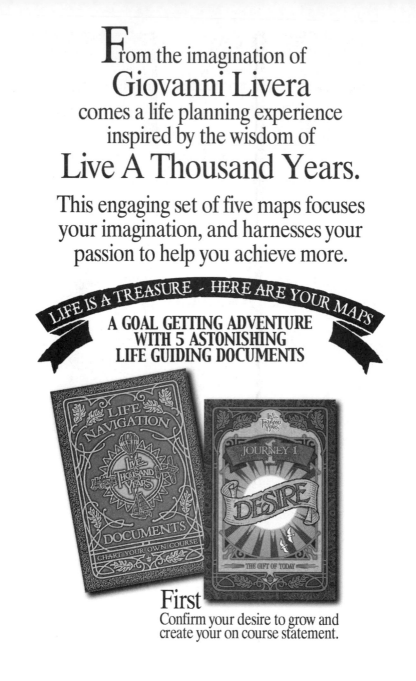

Frrom the imagination of
Giovanni Livera
comes a life planning experience
inspired by the wisdom of
Live A Thousand Years.

This engaging set of five maps focuses
your imagination, and harnesses your
passion to help you achieve more.

LIFE IS A TREASURE - HERE ARE YOUR MAPS

**A GOAL GETTING ADVENTURE
WITH 5 ASTONISHING
LIFE GUIDING DOCUMENTS**

First
Confirm your desire to grow and
create your on course statement.

Next
See your strengths and opportunities from a new perspective.

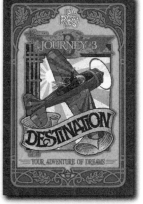

Then
Brainstorm possibilities for your bright future.

Anytime
Map a detailed action plan to achieve your best.

Always
Let go of what is holding you back and move forward living your dreams on schedule.

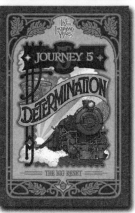

Chart your own course
and see how your story unfolds.

Now is the time to order your set of
Live A Thousand Years
Life Navigation Documents
at
TIMECOMPASS.com